CW00594388

APPLIQUÉ

THE Sew Quirky WAY

**FRESH DESIGNS FOR QUICK
AND EASY APPLIQUÉ**

MANDY MURRAY

DAVID & CHARLES

www.davidandcharles.com

Contents

Introduction

As you flip through the colourful pages of this book, my hope is that the quirky designs stop you in your tracks and cause your face to light up with a huge smile. I hope your mind starts to tick with all the creative possibilities. Imagine all the projects you could make for yourself or those you love, and know that you are treating yourself to sewing just for fun, for you!

This book is loaded with 12 appliqué patterns plus 12 projects that you can add the patterns to. You'll find instructions to create a cork bag, clutch, floor cushion, placemats, apron, insulated bag, circle tote and numerous wall-art pieces. All this, along with techniques to apply my appliqué designs to pre-made items too! You can mix and match the appliqués and projects to create your own combos. With all the possibilities appliqué possesses, you're only limited by your imagination.

My technique is a fused raw edge appliqué, with the edges of the fabric secured with gorgeous decorative machine stitches. The shapes that form my designs are layered on top of each other to build up a modern and unique take on a traditional technique. In this book you'll learn my methods for preparing, cutting and fusing appliqué together using an appliqué mat.

I must warn you here, my friends... appliqué is highly addictive. I take no responsibility for lack of housework or avoiding a night out on the town. I will insist that appliqué enhances your originality, inspiring you to be an artist with fabric and thread. I hope my words within the pages of this book give you confidence to continue to grow your skills in many aspects of the design process.

So, sit in a happy place, grab a cuppa and let me take you on a journey through my magical world of appliqué. Explore the many forms of this technique, discover my favourite supplies that will give you a fab finish, and enjoy every element in between! You'll learn how valuable stabilizers are, experiment with different feet for your sewing machine, and find that these often overlooked aspects of sewing can be surprisingly fun. I encourage you to trust your instincts with colour, rummage through your rainbow of scrap fabrics and turn them into textile art through my appliqué designs. This book is all about filling your soul with every feeling you enjoy about sewing.

Do you have built-in decorative stitches on your sewing machine and wonder what the heck to do with them? I'm here to help you see their value too! I'll inspire you to try them out in your appliqué, as they play a mega role in my style of sewing. There is nothing quite like seeing decorative stitches flow out from behind your needle, with shiny threads enhancing the design. This is my favourite part of the process, and I can get quite lost in the joy of stitching. This is why I love appliqué so much and I hope that I inspire you to sew for no other reason than your own mental and creative wellbeing – to sew for FUN and EXPRESSION. Now that is a rad reason to sew, don't you think?

Whether this is your first time encountering the wonderful world of appliqué or you've had experience with this technique, you'll find projects in this book you'll love! Feel free to start at any project that makes you smile the brightest, and refer back to the technique section in the front of this book. Enjoy, my lovelies, it's a pleasure to inspire you!

Tools & Materials

Appliqué gives you the option to keep it simple, requiring few supplies, or it has the power to explode your creativity like a party popper! It's adaptable for different styles and tastes, but most importantly it is loads of fun. Below, you'll find a list of necessary supplies along with fabrics and trims I think you'll enjoy working with. Check out the Suppliers list for details of how to get hold of some of the products I recommend.

Appliqué mat

If you've never used an appliqué mat before, you'll find my techniques a game changer! This is a MUST and you'll use it for every project in this book. There are many different appliqué mats on the market. You'll find Teflon and silicone versions, or check out the Sew Quirky appliqué mat (see Suppliers) – it's completely clear and the highest visibility. The amazing thing about an appliqué mat is that it will release the fusible web adhesive after it has been ironed to the mat so that the adhesive stays on the back of your fabrics (see Basic Fusible Appliqué Method).

Sewing machine

Of course! My sewing machine is my bestie when it comes to my style of appliqué. I absolutely love incorporating decorative stitches into my projects, especially to add texture and interest to my appliqué. The possibilities are endless when it comes to a sewing machine loaded with features and stitches. Please don't be discouraged if you have limited stitches on your machine. You'll find suggestions on how to make the most of simple stitches in the Rad Tips Before You Stitch section – and if you don't have a sewing machine at all, that's cool too. You might be a whizz at hand embroidery (see Hand Embroidery) and you can definitely apply your skills to my appliqué designs.

Machine needles

Topstitch needles are my favourite to use in my sewing machine. I recommend a size 80/12. Learn more about topstitch needles in Threads & Needles for a Sweet Result: Tips and ideas for using rayon thread.

Open toe presser foot

This foot provides a clear view of the stitching area and makes stitching appliqué SEW much easier! It is an absolute MUST! Learn more in Sewing Machine Feet & Tension.

Teflon, ¼in and zipper feet

These feet make techniques in this book a smooth and simple experience (see Sewing Machine Feet & Tension). Once you get the hang of these feet, you won't be able to live without them!

Iron + ironing surface

A mini iron is wonderful to use for appliqué, and having a portable ironing surface is great for moving around your sewing space.

Scissors

Small, sharp and pointy ones are perfect for cutting out your appliqué. A small round-tipped pair of scissors is vital for my appliquéd zipper technique.

Adhesives

When working with unusual materials such as vinyl, which can't be ironed from the top, an acid-free glue stick and double-sided tape come in super handy. Fray stop is a solvent-based, anti-fray adhesive that is great for preventing... you guessed it, fraying!

Rotary cutter, ruler and mat

I love using these tools for cutting precisely. Ensure you know how to use your rotary cutter safely.

Quilting clips

What's all the fuss about? Well, my friends, these clips are awesome for holding layers of fabric together effortlessly. The main reason I enjoy using them is that they won't mark your fabrics, which is particularly helpful when sewing vinyls and corks. Avoid using pins with these materials, as they leave permanent holes.

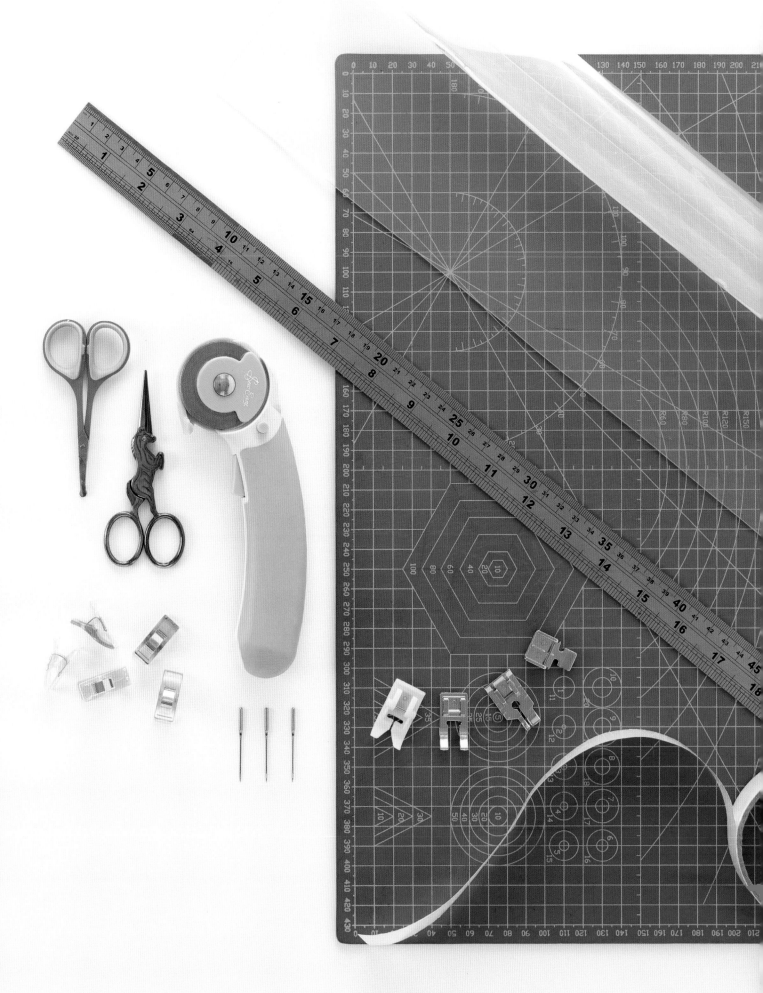

Fabric

Start with your pile of scrap cotton fabrics. Appliqué is a wonderful technique to make use of even the smallest piece of scrap fabric. It is not only resourceful but cost effective too! If you're looking to build your fabric stash, pre-cuts are a great option. Look out for unique and quirky novelty prints, as they are loads of fun to fussy cut (*see Fussy Cutting*).

Felt

100% wool felt is dreamy to work with and worth the extra expense. Wool felt can handle the heat when fused; it also doesn't pill like acrylic felt.

Vinyl

Vinyl comes in so many colours and textures, and it gives a project an absolute WOW factor. It can be daunting to work with at first, but with a few tricks and techniques you'll become confident in exploring this fun material!

Cork

An absolute joy to work with, cork fabric is vegan and eco-friendly. It sews like butter! It's light, plus water- and wear-and-tear resistant. It is an awesome alternative to leather. It's super easy to work with and makes projects look pretty damn schmick! Some cork fabrics on the market are thin with little body. Look out for cork fabric that has the same characteristics and hand feel as regular leather.

Raffia fabric

This versatile and highly textured fabric is a woven natural fibre. It is strong, yet soft and pliable to work with. Raffia gives a rustic and natural textural element to projects.

Fusible web

A paper backed, iron-on, sew-able, double-sided adhesive for bonding fabric together, fusible web is a product that varies in quality. There is an array of brands on the market, but my personal fave is Heat n Bond Lite (*see Suppliers*). It bonds fabrics without adding extra weight or stiffness. It doesn't 'gum up' the needle when sewing my layered appliqué designs and the paper also never separates from the adhesive prior to working with it (which, if it's happened to you, you'll know is an absolute nightmare). You never have that issue with Heat n Bond, so I highly recommend trying it!

Medium-weight fusible woven interfacing or tear-away

I use this in almost every project! It provides support to the fabrics behind my appliqué, preventing any puckering while stitching. Learn all about stabilizers and how important they are in *Keep Me Stable, Baby!*

Zipper

If you haven't tried continuous zipper, you don't know what you're missing out on! Continuous zipper has nylon teeth, making it extremely easy to work with. Not only can you cut it to your desired length with scissors or a rotary cutter, but you can sew directly over the nylon teeth. Sew Quirky offer some in stripes and rainbow colours (*see Suppliers*)!

Embellishments

Okay, so if it has a pompom, it's likely that I'll love it! Embellishing your projects with fab trims, tassels, fringing and pompoms of all sizes gives your work interest and, of course, QUIRK!

Webbing

Cotton webbing, in particular, looks beautiful made into straps and handles. Not only is it quick and easy, but it's strong too.

Eyelets, grommets and rivets

Eyelets stop the edge of a hole fraying and can be used to thread cords and ribbon through. You will see these used on the Rad & Fab backpack project. Along with eyelets, grommets and rivets, hardware gives handmade a professional look. You'll see grommets used on the Life's Short, Eat Donuts! apron.

Modern Appliqué Techniques

Layered Appliqué

Come and join me in my creative world of layered appliqué! My technique is a fused raw edge method, with the edges of the fabric secured with decorative machine stitches. The shapes are layered to build up a modern and unique take on traditional appliqué. Learn my methods for preparing, cutting and fusing your appliqué, and apply the following steps to all the projects in this book.

APPLIQUÉ PREPARATION METHOD

1. Trace and cut the pattern pieces

The appliqué pattern pieces for each project are provided in the Templates section at the end of this book. Printable versions can also be downloaded from www.davidandcharles.com (always check your printer settings to ensure that you are printing at full size). Please note that all pattern pieces are printed in reverse and should be traced this way onto the paper side of the fusible web. Simply lay the fusible web, paper side up, on top of the pattern pieces and trace with a pencil, leaving around ½in (1cm) between the pieces. Cut out all of the pieces from the fusible web, leaving approximately ¼in (6mm) excess around the outside of each piece (do not cut directly on the line at this stage).

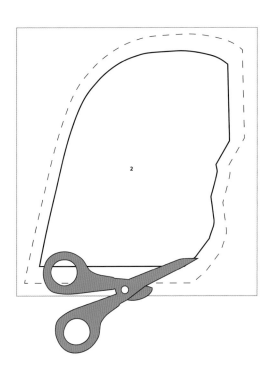

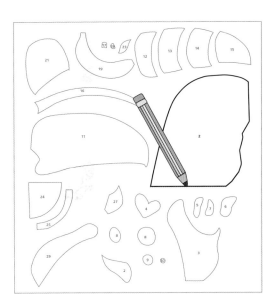

Remember to write the number on each shape before you cut it out!

2. Iron the pattern pieces onto fabric

Iron the pieces paper side up onto the wrong side of your chosen fabrics. If you're using glitter vinyl accents for any part of your appliqué, it's important to remember that these types of products can only be ironed on their wrong side, NEVER the right side.

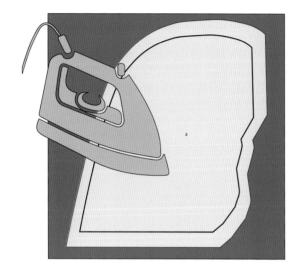

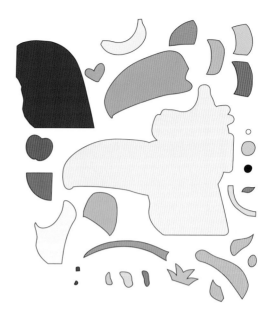

3. Cut the pieces out and prepare for assembly

Once the shapes are fused, cut out the pieces directly on the drawn lines. This gives the fabric a sealed edge.

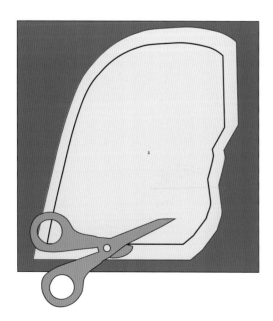

BASIC FUSIBLE APPLIQUÉ METHOD

1. Construct appliqué units

Each appliqué has its own Appliqué Placement Template provided on the pull-out sheet, which is a line drawing of the complete appliqué. Place the Appliqué Placement Template under an appliqué mat. If you're using a Sew Quirky appliqué mat, the template will grip slightly and hold in place. If your appliqué mat is slipping around, use some washi/masking tape to hold it in place.

Each appliqué pattern in this book outlines the order in which units need to be constructed. Once these units are assembled, it makes putting the whole appliqué together so much easier!

To construct a unit, remove the paper from the back of the fabric shape and position on top of the appliqué mat, with the right side of the fabric facing up (1a). When one appliqué piece goes under another, it will have a seam allowance. For correct placement, line up the outer edge that isn't touching another fabric piece (1b). Press with an iron for five seconds, until the fabric is fused to the appliqué mat. Do not over fuse, my friends, as this will burn the fusible web and it will lose its stick! If you're working with vinyl, use a glue stick to hold the vinyl piece onto the mat.

DO NOT IRON! Continue this method, applying each shape in numerical order, until you've fused all of the required units (1c).

1a

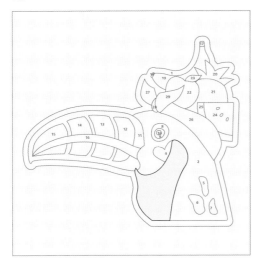

1b

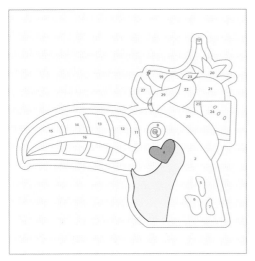

1c

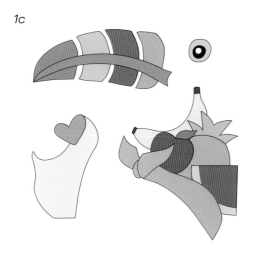

2. Flip / Fuse / Peel

This step is just to ensure that the shapes are fused together properly before you remove them from the appliqué mat. Note that this step isn't necessary with a Sew Quirky appliqué mat (*see Tools & Materials*). Carefully flip the appliqué mat over and fuse for a further five seconds.

Let the fused unit cool completely on the appliqué mat, then peel the unit off the mat in one piece, ready to fuse to the other units later. It is important to let the appliqué cool on the mat. Removing it while it's hot will result in the fusible web staying on the appliqué mat rather than on your fabric!

3. Put it all together!

Position the appliqué mat back over the Appliqué Placement Template. Start building the appliqué from shape number 1 (3a), all the way up until you reach the final piece (unless otherwise stated in the pattern) (3b). Gently flip the mat over and fuse from the back. Let it cool, then peel off the complete appliqué in one piece ready to fuse to your background.

3a

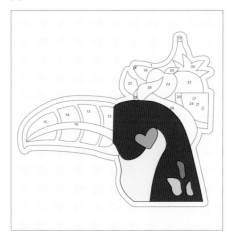

3b

Fabric Selection & Auditioning

For many, selecting fabrics can be one of the most intimidating parts of creating. My number one top tip to help with this phase of the design process is to work with a pre-cut fabric range. It gives you every print in a fabric designer's range, which means that the fabrics have been meaningfully designed to work together. This is a huge benefit in creating a coherent textile art. A 10in (25cm) pre-cut fabric bundle is a cost-effective and wonderful way to grow your stash.

Rummaging through fabric scraps is not only resourceful, but it reveals lots of creative possibilities! If you've been sewing for a while, I'm sure like many of us, your fabric scrap pile is starting to burst its banks. It's like a rainbow goldmine for finding just the right piece of fabric to finish off your appliqué perfectly. This is one of the reasons why I love appliqué. Not only are you able to reflect your unique style through design and colour, but you're also able to utilize scraps of fabric that might otherwise end up in landfill. That, my friends, is pretty damn cool. Art from scraps! When you appliqué with fabric scraps, you're guaranteed to produce work that's truly one of a kind. Cutting down on waste never looked so fab!

Now don't get me wrong: a boho vibe of clashing patterns and florals can look pretty cool, but it's definitely not everyone's cup of tea. Trying to incorporate a collection of super-busy prints is a huge challenge. Mixing solids or low-volume prints into your appliqué goes a long way towards achieving harmony within your work. Using solids behind highly patterned fabrics is a great way to emphasize and draw attention to a particular part of the design. It also allows a beautiful print to shine in all its glory! You can see an example of this in the fabrics used in the Alpaca My Bag! project.

How do I decide which fabric to use and where? Well, just like you I have prints I am instantly drawn to. Pick a favourite fabric that you're desperate to use. This is going to be our starting point and will help us throughout the process.

I like to lay out the Appliqué Placement Template (featuring the full image of the appliqué) in front of me. I start folding the fabrics I want to use and lay them roughly in the position of the shapes I am planning to cut from them. I take note of the colours in particular fabrics. Often, I am intentionally selecting a particular part of the fabric with the aim of tying the colours together. Repeating colours throughout an appliqué design creates a coherent vibe when it's viewed (or should I say admired?).

When I'm selecting fabrics, I always consider the little elements (each appliqué piece) as well as the big picture (the final piece). I like to repeat two or three colours throughout my work to create balance and movement, as this helps the viewer's eye to move around the entire piece. If you get stuck deciding on a colour, refer to that first fabric you picked... your favourite. Fabric can be a wonderful inspiration – not just for colour, but also for the decorative stitches you use with it.

At the end of the day, I encourage you to trust your instincts. Don't be afraid to push the boundaries with colour or texture. Don't let yourself get so bogged down with uncertainty, or lost in an indecisive funk, that you're unable to enjoy all the wonderful things about being creative. If you need a new perspective, snap a pic on your phone and see if everything is working together. If you're not vibing with a particular piece, it may be fighting or competing with other fabrics. Trace the appliqué piece again and try something new. Keep trying and experimenting with the creative process. Enjoy the ride!

Fussy Cutting

Growing a collection of fun and whimsical printed fabrics is a great way to add charm and interest to your piece of appliqué art! You may be thinking, what the heck is fussy cutting?! If you're new to the term, it simply means selecting a specific area of a print, rather than cutting randomly into the fabric. It is a cool technique for showcasing the design elements in your favourite fabrics.

When selecting fabric to fussy cut, consider the appliqué shape you're planning to feature it on. Avoid a shape that will have another shape layered on top of it that covers your beautiful motif. If you've gone to the effort of fussy cutting, you want maximum real estate! For example, if you've found a fabric with the sweetest bee print featured on it, choose to fussy cut it on the nose of a cute appliqué character. It will give the illusion of a bee landing on it and give an extra element to the design. Another example of this style of fussy cutting can be seen on the leaves featured in the Hanging with My Gnomies project, where I've intentionally selected areas of the fabric with the frog motif. Look closely and you'll see little snails fussy cut for the gnome's shoes too.

FUSSY CUTTING FOR PERFECT EYES

Eyes are probably the most important part of an appliquéd character. They create a focal point and your own eye is automatically drawn to them. So, let's make them fabulous with a few tips!

★ **Pupils** Fussy cut a fabric that features stars or metallic spots. It's a great alternative to adding a highlight and gives the eye a lovely glint.

★ **Eyes** Try to fussy cut from flower petals or fabrics with a watercolour vibe. These fabrics are great for adding interest and mystery, rather than a flat colour. Batik fabrics are also great for eyes, adding elements of texture with their organic form.

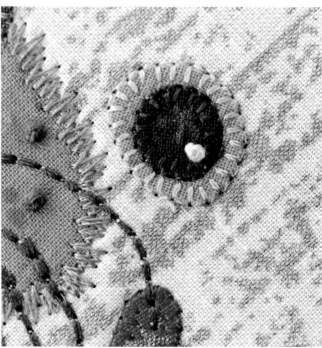

Appliqué on Cork & Vinyl

Working with unusual fabrics is loads of fun! It sets your projects apart and gives them a real point of difference. I enjoy using cork fabric and vinyl for bags and homewares, but I also LOVE featuring it in my appliqués too. Cork makes the perfect texture for a branch and glitter vinyl adds the all-important bling to a project!

CORK FABRIC

This is one of the coolest materials – it's vegan and eco-friendly and an absolute dream to work with. It is soft, pliable and has a unique texture. I'm a huge fan of the natural option, but it also comes in a rainbow of colours, even shimmery! Cork fabric can be fused from either side, but always treat the right side of the cork cautiously and keep heat to a minimum.

VINYL

Vinyls come in a huge rainbow of styles and colours, thicknesses and transparencies. They open up a whole world of sewing and I thoroughly enjoy all the creative possibilities they offer. Glitter and soft vinyls usually have a fabric backing and this allows them to be gently fused from the back, enabling you to iron your appliqué shapes and cut them out accurately. From there on, you will need to use either a glue stick or double-sided tape to hold the pieces in place, as no vinyl will handle being ironed from the front. It will simply melt, my friends, which will dull its sparkle.

BEST PRACTICE

There are a few things to keep in mind when working with these fabrics. Here are my top tips:

★ Quilting clips are perfect for holding these fabrics together. If you use pins, they will puncture the fabric and leave unsightly holes.

★ Double-sided tape or an acid-free glue stick are perfect for holding appliqué shapes in place.

★ Ensure your sewing machine is armed with a Teflon foot and a topstitch needle, and you'll be ready to show these fabrics who's boss!

Pieced Appliqué

If you love quilt making or improv piecing, you can incorporate them and create some pretty rad appliqué! This technique is based around the concept of creating your own fabric by stitching pieces together to add interest and individuality.

IDEAS FOR PIECED APPLIQUÉ

★ **Strips** Stitch strips of fabric together. Play with varying widths or keep them uniform. You can take it up a notch by cross-cutting the strips, rearranging them, and sewing them back together to create a checkerboard effect. You can get pretty fancy and cross-cut the pieced strips on a 60-degree angle by using the markings on your quilting ruler. This will give you a diamond pattern once sewn back together.

★ **Quilt blocks** If you're a quilter, it is highly likely that you have some random quilt blocks chillin' out somewhere that could be put to awesome use. For example, imagine an appliquéd pot or vase cut out from a quilt block. It would add an additional element to the design.

★ **Improv** Now this technique is the ultimate scrap buster! It can make the most amazing fabric and adds stacks of personality to appliqué. Check out the Be-Leaf in You project for an example of how to use this method.

TIPS FOR A SWEET FINISH

★ The most important thing when it comes to pieced appliqué is ensuring that your seams are pressed open to reduce bulk.

★ Ensure that your pieced fabric is pressed nicely. You may even like to use spray starch to get it crisp.

★ Once you cut your appliqué shape out, you could end up with some raw edges, particularly where there is a seam allowance. Add a small amount of fray stop to prevent these sections from fraying.

★ Select a decorative stitch, like a triple blanket stitch, that will make it easier to sew through the seam allowances in the piecing. A satin stitch also works well to conceal all the raw edges. Intricate decorative stitches may end up distorted, particularly going over seam allowances, so it's best to avoid these.

Rad Tips Before You Stitch!

Keep Me Stable, Baby!

We all need a little support, and so does your appliqué. Using stabilizer gives you smooth, professional results. The type of stabilizer you choose depends on the fabric and the nature of the project. It truly makes a world of difference.

INTERFACING HANDY DANDY TIPS

★ Rub interfacing between your fingertips and you'll feel the 'glue' side. Ensure this is facing the wrong side of your fabric.

★ Always read the instructions provided with each product and brand. Follow the manufacturer's recommendations to get the best result.

★ Once fused, wait for the fabric to cool before handling it. This enables the glue from the interfacing to set and bond.

Tear-away

This stabilizer provides temporary support that is generally easy to remove. It is cost effective and does the job! The main thing to consider when purchasing tear-away is that it varies in its 'tear-ability'. I'd suggest a light- to mid-weight tear-away that pulls cleanly from the stitches without damaging them. If more support is required, an additional layer of tear-away can be used. Tear-away is perfect for supporting appliqué on pre-made items such as denim jackets, vests, t-shirts and homewares. When using this product, I generally use pins to hold it in place. There are iron-on versions, but these are usually harder to remove from decorative stitching.

Medium-weight fusible woven interfacing

This is probably my favourite product for stabilizing appliqué. I might be a bit of an interfacing snob, but I ALWAYS choose woven. Why? Because whatever fabric you iron it onto will still feel and move like fabric. Fusible woven interfacing is a cotton fabric with one side coated with fusible glue. Once fused onto fabric it gives a slight thickness. I use this product on the wrong side of fine Liberty fabrics before adding fusible web. It gives them extra body and ensures that they aren't see-through.

Non-woven, firm, single-sided, fusible stabilizer

Look out for Decovil (*see Suppliers*) – this is a seriously cool product! It's a fusible interfacing with a leather-like (suede) feel. It is a beautiful option for bags, adding dimensional stability yet resisting bending. It is available in regular and light weights.

Fusible fleece

Use fusible fleece to add softness, body and stability. This single-sided fusible product gives fabric a beautiful, soft feel and adds a thick, lofty layer. It is lovely incorporated into bags and homewares. I enjoy using it in wall hangings too.

Bag wadding (batting)

Soft yet robust, this wadding (batting) is fantastic for projects such as bags, placemats and wall-art. It is thick and quite firm, but super-easy to sew by hand or machine. I use a non-fusible version, which you can hold in place with fabric adhesive spray if necessary.

Heavy-weight interfacing

This is a stiff interfacing perfect for adding loft and firmness. It can be used for bag bases, placemats and other textile projects. It is available as sew-in, single- and double-sided fusible. You can also find pre-cuts, such as the 16in (40.5cm) round placemat shapes that I used in the Totally Bee-licious project (*see Suppliers*). This product is machine washable too.

Reflective insulated lining

This is one coooool product! It will have your handmade products looking schmick! Not only could you make a reflective visor for your car, but also the most epic insulated grocery and lunch cooler bags EVER! It is easy to sew and machine washable. Your imagination is your only limit with this product. How about a robot costume and a rocket ship?

Sewing Machine Feet & Tension

Exploring different feet for your sewing machine can be surprisingly fun. There are usually loads of variations for each machine brand. I know, mention the word tension and some people freak out – but stay calm, my friends, and let me explain. Getting these things right makes certain tasks SEW much easier!

MY FAVE FEET (AND WHY THEY'RE FAB!)

Open toe foot

This foot provides a clear view of the stitching area and makes stitching appliqué a breeze! They do vary in size, so ensure that the stitching area is wide enough for the maximum stitch width on your sewing machine. The indentation on the bottom of the foot allows decorative stitching to glide under it and the centre marking is hugely useful too, allowing you to effortlessly align the centre of the foot with the edge of the appliqué shapes.

If your open toe foot doesn't have a centre marking, use a permanent marker or a small amount of red nail polish to make one.

¼in foot

Accurate seams really do matter and achieving a perfect ¼in (6mm) seam is a cinch with one of these feet. If you haven't tried it, give it a go and see for yourself how neat and accurate your results are, every time.

Teflon foot

Show vinyl, plastic and leather materials who's boss with this coated foot! This foot is designed to prevent tricky fabrics from sticking to the bottom of the foot. Sewing with a Teflon foot makes working with these fabrics a dream.

Zipper foot

This foot comes in handy not just for inserting a zipper. It allows the needle to stitch close to trims and cording without the pressure of the foot getting in the way. Most sewing machines come with a zipper foot as standard.

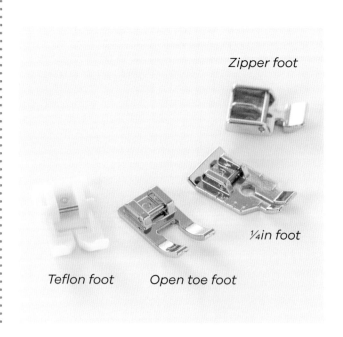

Zipper foot

¼in foot

Teflon foot

Open toe foot

TENSION

I was once a scaredy cat about adjusting tension and simply avoided it, mostly because I didn't understand it. Once it sinks in, you'll wonder why the heck you were worried about it. Before we dive into the world of tension, it's important to eliminate other issues...

Checklist before you touch tension

★ Ensure your machine is threaded correctly. Pay particular attention to the top thread, making sure that it is snugly between the tension discs.

★ Check that nothing is stopping the top thread from falling freely off the spool.

★ Is your bobbin inserted correctly? It should also be wound evenly and at proper tension. Never wind a bobbin at super-high speed, as this often causes a spongy bobbin.

★ Now tell the truth... how long has it been since you changed your needle? As a rough guide, it should be changed when you start a new project or after about eight hours of sewing.

★ Keep it clean! Dirt in your machine can cause havoc with its performance. Ensure there are no loose threads stuck between the tension discs or in the bobbin area.

★ Has it been a while since you treated your machine to a service? You want it running at its best, so you can enjoy working on it without any issues.

Tension plays a massive role in the finished result of your appliqué. So, let's start off with my number one tip on this topic: take a photo or write down your current settings. Why? I want you to have a play with the tension on your machine so that you can understand how it works. I don't want you to be afraid of it. You have noted your current settings, so it's no sweat to go back to them.

Now the main aim of the game – you want to avoid any 'bobbin dots' or loops on the top of your appliqué. When your sewing machine has balanced tension, both the top and bottom threads flow evenly, producing a symmetrical stitch. For appliqué, my preference is for the top thread tension to be looser, causing the top thread colours to be slightly visible on the back. This guarantees that no bobbin thread or fill is making an appearance centre stage on the front of your appliqué.

Let's do a little test!
Here is what you'll need:

- Bobbin wound with bobbin fill (learn more about bobbin fill on the following pages)

- Coloured top thread

- Scrap of black fabric with interfacing or tear-away stabilizer (*see Keep Me Stable, Baby!*) on the back

Set your machine to a zigzag stitch and sew a line of stitching. Take a look at the results. If bobbin thread is visible on the top side, the top tension is too tight. Lowering the top tension will often decrease the pressure on the thread, allowing the bobbin and top thread to relax together on the back of your stitching. Don't be afraid to keep testing and experimenting until you achieve a nice finish. Keep in mind that thread weights effect the tension. So it's a good idea to keep notes indicating the thread brand, size and type, plus the number on the upper tension.

If you continue to have tension issues with your machine, it may be necessary to adjust the bobbin spring. Refer to your sewing machine manual or take your baby to a specialist machine tech to get it jusssstttt right!

Threads & Needles for a Sweet Result

Let's talk about threads, baby. Let's talk about all the good things thread gives to your projects. For any thread lover, finding a store loaded with thread racks is like walking into a candy store – it's a whole new world, filled with diversity! I share my favourites below, but I also encourage you to experiment with different weights and styles of thread.

Now before we dive into the wonderful world of threads, let's start off with what thread to wind around the bobbin. It may only be visible on the back, but it is still hugely important.

BOBBIN FILL

I'd like to introduce you to my good friend, bobbin fill. It is my absolute go-to for appliqué sewing. Now by no means is this a good choice for piecing or garment sewing, so please do not use it for construction. It is light-weight, fine and enjoys hanging out with embroidery threads for a stroll around your appliqué. It is the perfect choice when it comes to embroidery and decorative stitching. I mostly only ever use white, but it is also available in black.

Why I love bobbin fill

★ Bobbin fill is inexpensive. Its fineness means that you can fit loads of meterage on your bobbin, resulting in less time wasted reloading your bobbin. Happiness is a full bobbin, don't you agree?

★ Combined with shiny or textured embroidery thread, bobbin fill does an awesome job at balancing your tension, allowing your top thread to take form and lie nicely on top of your appliqué. This gives your stitching a more dimensional effect.

★ There is no need to change your bobbin to match your top thread.

★ The fineness of bobbin fill reduces bulk and is soft against your skin, which is nice when appliquéing items you'll wear.

★ Bobbin fill in combination with embroidery threads creates an intentional imbalance when it comes to the tension on your machine. You see, it works in your favour and allows the top embroidery thread to be pulled to the wrong side of the stitching. This ensures that your bobbin thread is not visible on the right side of your work.

★ You can purchase pre-wound bobbins, but make sure they will fit your machine. I personally invested in extra bobbins for my machine and wind a whole bunch of them at once. I store them in a bobbin case and then I'm always ready to roll!

★ In my experience, some sewing machines will be fussy with certain brands of bobbin fill. Find one that works for you.

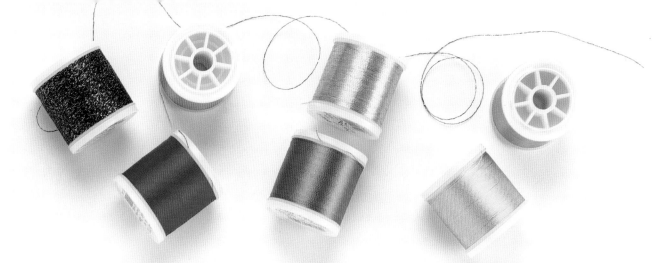

THREAD, GLORIOUS THREAD!

There is nothing quite like seeing your decorative stitches flow out behind your needle, with the shiny threads enhancing the design. Now I am all for buying trims, buttons and even fabric at the op shop (charity shop or thrift store), but threads are not something I'd recommend buying second-hand. Quality threads play a huge role not only in looks, but also in the performance of your sewing machine, so it's one of those things where it's worth investing in quality. Start off with some of your favourite colours and gradually build your collection. Some thread brands are available as a starter kit too.

There's a whole jungle of threads on the market, but my favourite is rayon 40 weight. Note that the higher the weight, the finer the thread. The brand Madeira receives a gold glitter star from me – stitching with it is always a positive experience with beautiful results. Embroidery threads add extraordinary brightness and define the stitching. Quality rayon thread has a high tensile strength, exceptional running abilities and optimum colour fastness to give longevity and consistency. There are many quality brands on the market, so find one that works for you. You can also get metallic, twist and variegated threads to add even more interest and richness to your work.

Tips and ideas for using rayon thread

★ Do not be tempted to use rayon threads for construction. They are weaker in comparison to regular sewing threads.

★ Change your needle. A topstitch needle is my go-to. The eye and the scarf (the flat bit above the eye) are significantly different to those found on a regular needle. Like an embroidery needle, the topstitch variety has a larger eye. This prevents breakage and fraying and puts less pressure on the embroidery thread.

★ Any 'bling' lover will want to try metallic threads. However, these can be a little tricky to work with. Make sure you have a fresh needle in your machine, and have a play. You may need to use a thread net to stop the thread falling off the spool too fast. Avoid sewing too quickly or using complex decorative stitching, as it can cause issues.

★ If you're wondering whether you can use cotton threads to appliqué, of course you can! The result will be a matte finish.

★ Try different weights of thread. I enjoy using 40 weight thread, especially with bolder stitch choices. It gives a lovely finish along the edge of the appliqué. If you decide to try a thicker thread, it's likely that you'll need to adjust your tension, and I'd recommend avoiding very intricate decorative stitches.

★ Variegated threads can be a real buzz! However, I'm not a huge fan of those varieties that have a very predictable pattern, causing distinct stripes of colour that are noticeable in your stitching. Look for those that have a more gradual or natural change in colour. This thread is fab for appliquéing around leaves or feature points.

★ Test it, babe! Grab some scraps of fusible appliqué shapes and fuse them to a sample piece of your background, then give it a try.

Oh Sew Glam Decorative Stitching

Do you have built-in decorative stitches on your sewing machine and wonder what the heck to do with them? I'm here to help you see their value and inspire you to try them out in your appliqué. Decorative stitches play a mega role in my style of sewing.

Decorative stitching is pretty magical if you ask me. One can be hypnotized by the needle flowing through the thread, the fabric and leaving a trail of beauty behind.... As much as I love illustrating my designs and playing with colour, it is through the stitching of my appliqué that I truly get lost in my creative world. I'm so focused on the formation of the stitch that everything else in my mind disappears. I cut off from everyday stresses and go with the flow of the stitch. I urge you to try it: to sew for the pure joy of it!

Tips for achieving fab results

★ An open toe foot on your sewing machine will be your best friend when appliquéing with decorative stitches. This foot will give you clear vision and will also help you line up your stitch with the edge of the appliqué (*see Sewing Machine Feet & Tension*).

★ Apply what you learnt about tension (*see Sewing Machine Feet & Tension*). It may be beneficial to lower your upper thread tension to prevent the bobbin thread pulling up to the top.

★ Sew more slowly and be patient. I know this can be hard. I often lower the speed control on my machine to keep me from getting too excited! This will ensure the correct stitch formation.

★ Most sewers are used to sewing fast and straight, pushing the fabric through the machine. If you stick with this technique while sewing decorative stitches, you'll be so disappointed with the results. You'll end up with random gaps in the design or you may hardly recognize the stitch you selected. The more lightly you hold the fabric and let the machine feed your fabric through at its own pace, the better the stitch will form and the happier you'll be with your work.

★ Decorative stitches don't sew straight – the needle often moves right, left and backwards to create each stitch. WATCH THE FOOT! The presser foot is the best guide for the placement of the stitch. Keep the centre marking of the foot along the edge of the appliqué.

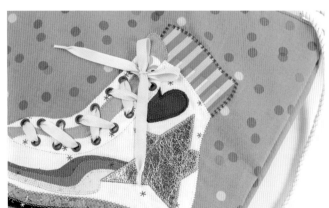

★ Watch how the stitch is formed and you will soon notice that each stitch has a pivot point. At this point, you can realign your foot with the direction of the appliqué shape without distorting the stitch.

★ Some appliqué shapes require the decorative stitch to meet up where you started. Therefore, select a decorative stitch that will blend when it meets the beginning point, just in case it doesn't quite match up.

★ Keep in mind how detailed the decorative stitch is and make decisions on the type of thread and its weight accordingly. Thicker or metallic threads don't enjoy very detailed stitches.

★ Some stitches aren't so fab for appliqué. Hollow or open stitches of flowers or motifs, although pretty cool, don't work so well as they get lost in the appliqué. They also don't conceal the raw edges of the appliqué.

★ Layer your stitching just like your appliqué. Start with shape number 1. Sometimes, if I want to sew numerous shapes in the same colour thread I'll break this 'rule'.

SEWING MACHINES ARE AWESOME!

Many sewing machines have the capability to sew a single stitch pattern. This means you can program the machine to automatically tie off after one stitch pattern. I use this feature regularly for adding a star or flower stitch in the centre of the eye 'glint', or on its own on top of the pupil for more detail. I usually sew this highlight in white thread, but you could take the 'glint' to the next level with a shimmery metallic thread. Play with this feature; I've used it for nostrils and eyelashes too.

Peruse your instruction manual for some of these other wonderful features I enjoy using...

★ **Mirror image** Changes the orientation of a stitch.

★ **Flip** Flips the stitch from top to bottom.

★ **Stitch designer** Allows you to create your very own stitch or modify existing stitches. This is one of my favourite features on my Bernette sewing machine. Patterns can be created by free-hand drawing on the touch screen or by tapping points on the grid. If you don't have a furry stitch, but you have a stitch designer feature, you can create your very own! Check out my tutorial for this on my YouTube channel (*see About the Author*).

Create a stitch sampler

The best way to learn which decorative stitches tickle your fancy is to create a stitch sampler. It's a good idea to stitch them all out, as the little image in your instruction manual can be deceiving. You can make your sampler as fancy or as basic as you wish, but I recommend that you note down the stitch number, plus its length and width. Keep your stitch sampler with your sewing machine for easy reference. When stitching your sampler, don't be afraid to adjust the lengths and widths of stitches. The sky's the limit! You'll end up with a collection of stitches that you love working with – and if your sewing machine has a memory, you'll be able to save your favourites so that they're all together.

To get started, try finding my most used decorative stitches on your machine. Don't get caught up trying to match your stitch identically to mine, just find something similar. Before I forget, the most important thing... is to have FUN! There is no need for perfection; embrace a give-it-a-go attitude and celebrate your achievement. Always remember that your skills will grow with practice.

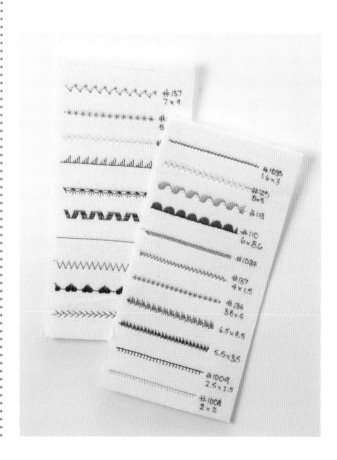

Simple Stitches

As much as an appliqué adorned with an array of decorative stitches is pretty cool, I don't want those without all the mod cons to miss out. So if your sewing machine doesn't have a ton of fancy stitches, please find some ideas and alternatives below.

★ **Simple straight stitch** You can either sew 'regularly' or 'free-motion'. Sewing over the straight stitching numerous times creates an awesome sketchy look.

★ **Triple straight stitch** Great for outlining and giving definition.

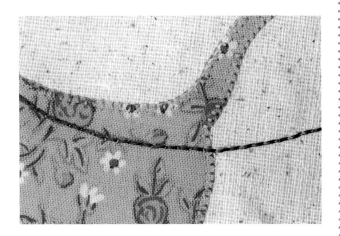

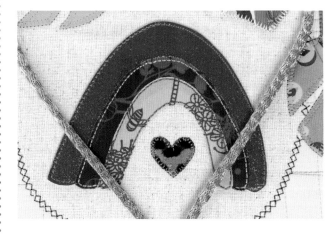

★ **Zigzag** Experiment with different density all the way up to a satin stitch.

To compensate for not having many stitch options, make other elements of the design process stand out. Use variegated threads or overlap simple stitches with different colours. Use bold fabrics or embellish parts of your appliqué with hand embroidery, beads or sequins (*see Make It Shine with Embellishments*).

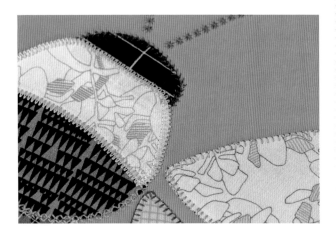

Hand Embroidery

There are stacks of hand-embroidered decorative stitches – and YES you could totally apply them as an alternative to machine sewing around your appliqué. It will be more time consuming, but who cares!

This style of sewing is all about relaxing and doing something that's fun, for you. I like to incorporate little touches of hand embroidery, mostly French knots as glints in eyes or freckles. Backstitching is a great way to give characters more emotion by adding eyebrows or dimples. Check out the dinosaur in the You Are Dino-mite project to see this technique in practice, and the Otterly Adorable project for the otter's backstitched whiskers and French knot freckles.

Use these helpful stitch diagrams below if you'd like to add more dimension to your appliqués.

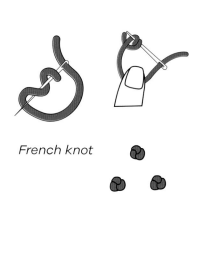

French knot

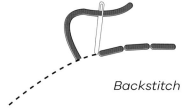

Backstitch

Make It Shine with Embellishments!

When it comes to the embellishing stage of a project, my mind gets wayyy too excited – it seems to bring my creativity to a peak! I think this feeling is triggered by digging through my retro suitcase, in which I store the trims, tassels and pompoms that I've found on my adventures.

Some of these treasures I found in 'op shops', also known as charity or thrift stores, when I was a kid. I've been growing my collection for quite some time! Certain trims bring back memories of when I found them, but that is what is so special about handmade.

Don't get me started on my button collection... My first memory of buttons is sitting on the floor, rummaging through my mum's vintage container with my little sister. We would pick out our favourites, our fingers hunting them as they tried to bury themselves. I could spend hours looking at buttons, wondering about the outfits they once adorned. The thrill of finding the perfect pair for the wheels on the Rad & Fab backpack was such a simple yet satisfying feeling!

Tips to grow a collection full of happiness

★ Hit up the op shops, charity or thrift stores. They usually have a craft section where you'll discover random bits and bobs. You never know what you'll find, perhaps the perfect buttons or trim to make your project one-of-a-kind. Look out for jars of buttons filled with lots of colours and shapes.

★ Browse vintage or antique stores. Although usually at a higher price point, the likelihood of finding something fab is equally high. Cool brooches or vintage embroidered patches are a great way to take your project to another level.

★ Visit craft and quilting stores. Keep your eyes peeled: you never know what might be hiding in the nooks and crannies of these stores.

★ Create your own. YES! This is such a cool way to make the perfect embellishment. Making your own tassel from vinyls or leather allows you to match or contrast perfectly. The same goes for pompoms. Get yourself a pompom maker, gather up some wool in your fave colours and experiment.

★ Try dollar stores and pound shops. As a craft-loving kid, an adventure to the 'cheap' shop with my mum was better than any candy shop for me! We would hit up the craft aisle and find loads of goodies. Look out for packs of pompoms which can add a quirk to your work, or jumbo pompoms on keychains. Don't forget the hardware section – you might just find funky chain or cord for bag straps.

Tips for attaching embellishments

★ Fabric glue is okay, but stitched is best! Pompoms can be attached with a small amount of craft glue, and then sewn through the middle to secure with a single stitch.

★ Tacking (basting) is your friend. Tacking your trims in place is well worth the time. There is nothing worse than turning your project the right way out and feeling that disappointment when the trim has moved and missed the seam.

★ Your zipper foot is one handy sole! This foot makes sewing on trims, especially mini pompom trim, so much easier. It allows the needle to get close to the trim without the foot getting in the way.

★ Grab a cuppa, find a relaxing space and get your hand stitchin' on! Some trims are easier to attach by hand, especially for trims with beading etc.

★ Did you know that many sewing machines can sew buttons on? It is usually a stitch within the buttonhole section. There is also a button speciality foot! It is great because it attaches buttons very securely. Of course, it isn't smart enough to sew on shank buttons – you'll need to do those by hand.

Quilting & Finishing Techniques

To do justice to your fab appliqué, you need to think about how you handle the background and how you are going to display your creation to the world. To quilt or not to quilt? Will you frame or hang your finished work? Here are some ideas.

QUILTING

There are so many quilting options out there. It's one of the techniques that you can keep simple or go all out! It really is up to personal preference if you add quilting or not, but it does add a whole different textural element. Here are some ideas to fire up your quilting mojo.

★ Straight-line quilting is achievable and modern. Try swapping thread colours and varying line widths for different effects.

★ Remember those decorative stitches we spoke about using? Well my friend, you can rock these in quilting backgrounds too! The background can end up being just as interesting as your appliqué.

★ Echo quilting is simply stitching around the outside of your appliqué numerous times and gradually making your way out to the edge of your background fabric. It's great for drawing focus to your textile art.

★ Free-motion quilting is one of my favourites. Fill in the background space with swirls, 'pebbles' or floral details. It is a creative outlet all on its own! This technique is loads of fun and your skills will only bloom with practice.

★ Hand quilting adds a beautiful organic feel to your work, not to mention the zen of mindful quilting with needle and thread.

FINISHING TECHNIQUES

How you choose to display your textile art greatly changes the overall look, and through the projects in this book you'll find an array of finishing techniques. Choosing a finishing technique that complements the design is key, whether you decide to bind a wall art piece, pop it in a frame, stretch it over a canvas or get funky with a wooden hoop. Try painting a frame or hoop with a pop of colour and then add pompoms too if you're an addict like me! You'll see an example of this in the Prickly Positivi tea project.

Binding

When it comes to binding the edges of a piece, try a facing technique as displayed on the Be-Leaf in You project. It's a lovely finishing technique that is crisp and lets the appliqué remain the star of the show.

GETTING PROFESSIONAL-LOOKING RESULTS

You owe it to your fabulous appliqué, and to yourself, to finish your projects in a high-quality way. Here are my top hints.

Topstitching

Add topstitching for a gorgeous finish. This step is worth the extra effort and time. Not only does it add a decorative element, but it also enhances the robustness and durability of your work. Try highlighting certain features of your sewing with topstitching. Here are some tips for achieving schmick topstitching:

★ Ensure you have a topstitch needle in your machine. It is super sharp and will pierce through the fabric layers smoothly.

★ Lengthen your stitch length to 3 or 3.5mm.

★ Flatten out the seams and give your project a thorough press.

★ Adjust the needle position to get nice and close to the edge of your work, usually with ⅛in (3mm) seam allowance.

Choosing hardware

Bag hardware, rivets and grommets also give your projects a really snazzy look. There's a huge variety of hardware options, in an array of colours and with many purposes. When you pick out your hardware, select something that complements your creation. It is all about enhancing your project. I personally like to stick with the same metal colour throughout each project.

Otterly Adorable

This appliqué wall art is seriously like no otter! But I must warn you, hanging this cutie on your wall may result in an excessive number of potentially repetitive compliments: "AWWW-TTER!". Vinyl isn't your thing? No worries, you can totally use regular fabric as an alternative.

You will need

- **Machine feet:** Open toe foot and Teflon foot
- 16 x 22in (40.5 x 56cm) linen fabric, for background
- 16 x 22in (40.5 x 56cm) medium-weight woven fusible interfacing
- 16 x 17in (40.5 x 43cm) iron-on fusible web
- 10in (25cm) square, iridescent vinyl transparent, for water ripples
- Two 10in (25cm) squares, coordinating brown cotton fabrics, for body and ears
- Two 10in (25cm) squares, coordinating cream and mustard cotton fabrics, for head and tail
- 8in (20cm) square, printed cotton fabric, for belly
- Three 5in (13cm) squares, orange, citron and green glitter vinyl, for floaties (arm bands)

- 5in (13cm) square, rust cotton fabric, for arms
- 3in (7.5cm) square, mustard cotton fabric, for behind nose
- Five 2in (5cm) squares, red, pink, green, navy and blue cotton fabrics, for cheeks, nose, nostrils and eyes
- 2in (5cm) square, navy wool felt, for claws
- Rust, olive and white stranded embroidery thread (floss), for whiskers, freckles and pupil highlights
- Co-ordinating embroidery threads to match appliqué
- 12 x 16in (30 x 40.5cm) canvas, matching frame and staple gun
- Appliqué mat
- Glue stick
- Double-sided tape

Finished size: 12 x 16in (30 x 40.5cm)

CUTTING

Linen fabric
Cut one rectangle, 16 x 20in (40.5 x 50cm).

Medium-weight woven fusible interfacing
Cut one rectangle, 16 x 20in (40.5 x 50cm).

Fuse to the wrong side of the linen rectangle.

Iridescent vinyl
This vinyl often has a thin protective layer of plastic. Leave this layer on the vinyl and trace the water ripples onto it using a marker pen. Cut out the shapes and then remove the plastic.

CONSTRUCTION

1. Refer to *Modern Appliqué Techniques* at the beginning of this book and use the placement template provided to select your fabrics. Cut them out using the Otterly Adorable reversed appliqué pieces and the table below.

1, 7, 23, 26	floaties	orange glitter vinyl
24, 27	pineapple	citron glitter vinyl
25, 28	pineapple top	green glitter vinyl
3, 6, 9, 10	body & ears	brown fabrics
2, 8	arms	rust fabric
4, 11, 13	tail, head & behind nose	mustard fabrics
17, 18	heart cheeks	red fabric
12	mouth	pink fabric
14	nose	green fabric
5, 15, 16, 20, 22	belly, nostrils & inner eyes	navy fabric
19, 21	outer eyes	blue fabric
29, 30	claws	navy wool felt

During the fusible appliqué process, please be mindful when working with heat-sensitive materials like vinyl. Often products such as glitter vinyl, which have a fabric backing, can be ironed gently from the back; however, they should NEVER be ironed from the right side. Always test your product first before diving into your project. You'll be otterly disappointed if you melt your piece of textile art!

2. Use the *Layered Appliqué* instructions to construct the eye and nose units of the otter following the number order shown. Use shapes 12–16 for the nose unit and shapes 19–22 for the eyes. Use a glue stick to build the pineapple floaties 23–28.

3. Once you have prepared the eye, nose and pineapple floatie units, fuse all the otter units together on the appliqué mat, starting from shape number 1 (remember not to fuse the glitter vinyl) and building the units up until you reach shape number 22. Leave the claws and the pineapple floatie units off until later.

4. Place the large oval of iridescent vinyl in position on top of the placement template, followed by the otter unit. Stick double-sided tape onto the iridescent vinyl where the otter overlaps it to hold together. Place another section of double-sided tape on the back of the iridescent vinyl, only in the area where the otter is so that it will not be visible later.

5. Position the otter in the centre of the linen background, landscape orientation. You can place a couple of pins in the belly section to hold it, but do not pierce the vinyl as it will leave permanent pin holes. Carefully fuse the fabric sections, particularly the head, legs and tail, with the tip of an iron.

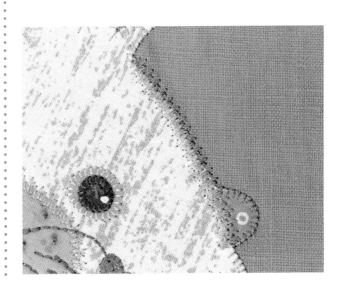

6. I'm otterly excited – it's time to sew! Use these stitch suggestions as inspiration:

★ Head (avoiding the fluffy hair sections), tail and behind nose: use a 'furry'-look stitch, grass stitch or zigzag with approximately 6mm stitch width.

★ Legs, arms, fluffy hair and vinyl water: use a 2 x 2mm blanket stitch.

★ Heart cheeks, ears, eyes, mouth, nose and nostrils: use a 1.5 x 1.5mm blanket stitch.

★ Belly: use a 4 x 4mm star stitch.

7. Use a glue pen or double-sided tape to attach the pineapple floatie units, then sew with these stitches:

★ Floaties: use a 2 x 2mm blanket stitch.

★ Pineapples: use a 2.5mm straight stitch. Sew seven or eight lines of stitching through the pineapple.

It's important to keep in mind the vinyl elements of this appliqué. I highly recommend using a Teflon-coated (non-stick) foot for areas where the foot will be touching vinyl. Your regular foot may stick and grip to the vinyl, causing your sewing machine to stitch inconsistently. I also suggest keeping the stitching fairly simple for these elements.

8. Position the claws on the feet to create a webbed look. Use a glue pen to hold them in place, then stitch as follows:

★ Claws: use a 2mm straight stitch. Sew one line of stitching through the middle of each claw.

9. Lay the remaining ripples of iridescent vinyl in position. The easiest way to hold these in place is to use a couple of pins to push up and over the vinyl and back down through the fabric (avoiding piercing the vinyl). This will hold them just enough for you to start sewing.

★ Ripples: use a 2 x 2mm blanket stitch or a regular straight stitch.

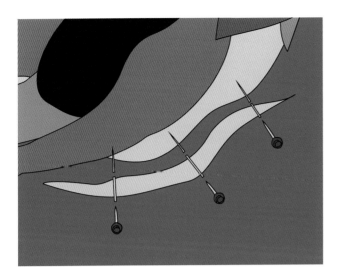

It is easier to start halfway down one side of the vinyl, rather than at the point.

10. This cutie needs some whiskers! You have two options:

★ Whisker option 1 (sewing machine): use a 3mm x 3mm triple stitch.

★ Whisker option 2 (hand embroider): use three strands of stranded embroidery thread (floss) for back stitch (*see Hand Embroidery*).

11. French knots are worth the effort! See *Hand Embroidery* and add the following:

★ Highlights: using two strands of white stranded embroidery thread (floss), make a French knot (two wraps of needle) highlight in each pupil.

★ Freckles: using three strands of olive stranded embroidery thread (floss), make six French knots (three wraps of the needle) for the freckles on either side of the nose.

12. Carefully give your textile art a press with an iron from the wrong side. Place it in the centre of the canvas. Using a staple gun, secure the piece in the middle of each long side first, carefully pulling the fabric taut as you go, but ensuring the appliqué stays central. Then secure in the middle of each short side.

If a framed canvas isn't your thing, you can make your new otter friend into a basic tote or even a cushion.

13. Continue to staple every inch (2–3cm) or so, making sure to pull tightly on the material so that it doesn't pucker and the front is smooth. Leave about 2in (5cm) from the corners unstapled.

14. Fold one side of the fabric around the corner and tuck in place under the fabric (you may need to trim any excess). Fold the remaining edge of fabric over itself so that it's flush with the edge of the canvas and staple in place. Repeat for the remaining corners.

15. Trim any excess fabric and cover the edges with masking tape for a nice finish. Frame if desired.

Hang or gift to someone who is otterly amazing!

Hanging with My Gnomies

There is nothing better than hanging with your gnomie! Their furry friends love joining them for walks too. These garden gnomes add a sense of magical whimsy to any space. Create this quirky floor cushion and add charm to any room.

You will need

- **Machine feet:** Regular sewing foot and open toe foot
- 36 x 17in (91 x 43cm) iron-on fusible web
- 45 x 44in (115 x 112cm) Osnaburg or equivalent upholstery-weight linen fabric, for gusset and base
- 24 x 44in (61 x 112cm) patterned fabric, for top
- 72 x 44in (170 x 112cm) medium-weight woven fusible interfacing
- Four 10in (25cm) squares, variety of skin-coloured fabrics, for bodies
- Four 10in (25cm) squares, green floral fabrics, for cat and dogs
- 10in (25cm) square, citron fabric, for stems
- Four 5in (13cm) squares, strawberry print fabrics, for hats
- Four 5in (13cm) squares, floral fabrics, for shirts and dress
- Twelve 5in (13cm) squares, solid fabrics in a variety of colours, for beards, hair, shoes, shorts, flowers and leaves
- 24in (61cm) continuous zipper (optional)
- 3½ cubic ft (100ltr) stuffing or bean bag filling
- Co-ordinating embroidery threads to match appliqué
- Sewing thread for construction to match base fabric
- Four mini pompoms
- Appliqué mat
- Double-sided tape, ¼in (6mm) wide
- Round-tipped scissors

Finished size: 21 x 21in (53.5 x 53.5cm)

CUTTING INSTRUCTIONS

Osnaburg, patterned fabric and medium-weight woven fusible interfacing

Cut a 23in (59cm) square from each fabric and two from the interfacing. Fold them into quarters, position the 21½in (53.5cm) quarter circle pattern piece provided on each one in turn, with the straight edges on the fold, and draw around it. Cut out, then fuse the interfacing to the wrong side of the fabrics.

Osnaburg and medium-weight woven fusible interfacing

Cut two 10 x 34½in (25 x 87.5cm) strips of both Osnaburg and interfacing, for the gusset. Fuse the interfacing to the wrong side of the Osnaburg.

Fussy cut shapes to add more interest. Fit a snail on a shoe, a mouse on the shirt or a frog on a leaf. See Modern Appliqué Techniques: Fussy Cutting to find out how.

CONSTRUCTION

1. Refer to *Modern Appliqué Techniques* at the beginning of this book and use the placement template provided to select your fabrics. Cut them out using the Hanging with My Gnomies reversed appliqué pieces and the table below.

Gnome A, B & C		
1, 4, 9, 12	body	darker skin-coloured fabrics
2, 5	shoes	navy fabric
3, 6	shorts	blue, red & teal fabric
7, 10	shirt	floral fabrics
8	beard	orange, pink & citron fabric
11	hat	strawberry fabric
Gnome D		
1, 3, 6, 7, 9	body	light skin-coloured fabric
2, 4	shoes	navy fabric
5	dress	patterned fabric
8	heart	pink fabric
10	hair	blue fabric
11	hat	strawberry fabric
Flowers (x2)		
1, 3	leaves	green fabrics
2	stems	citron fabric
4, 5, 6, 7, 8, 9, 10, 11	flower	rainbow solid fabrics
Cat & Dogs	variety of green patterned fabrics	

2. Use the *Layered Appliqué* instructions to construct units of the gnomes and flowers following the number order shown. Use shapes 1A–12A for the Gnome A unit, shapes 1B–12B for the Gnome B unit, shapes 1C–12C for the Gnome C unit, shapes 1D–11D for the Gnome D unit and shapes 1F–11F for the two flower units.

3. Once you have prepared the above units along with the cat and dogs, fuse them onto the two strips of Osnaburg, positioning them 1in (2.5cm) from the base and reserving one flower unit until step 5.

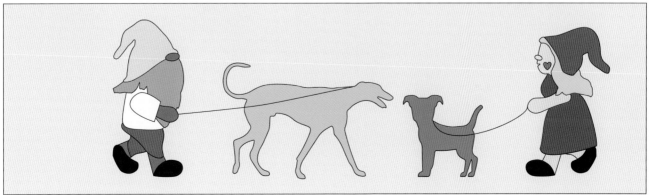

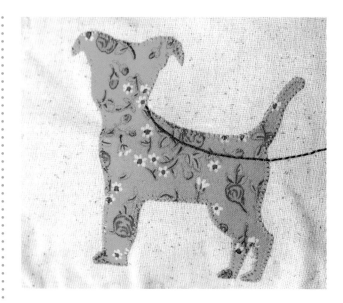

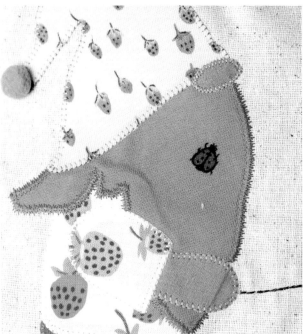

4. Let's stitch, gnomie! Give your gnomes character with fun decorative stitches (*see Oh So Glam Decorative Stitches*). Use the following as a guide:

★ Body, shoes, shorts, shirts, hats, hair, dogs, cat and flower: use a 2 x 2mm blanket stitch.

★ Beards: use a 'furry'-look stitch, grass stitch or zigzag with approximately 4mm stitch width.

★ Dress: use a 3.5 x 3.5mm flower stitch.

★ Leaf: use a 2 x 4mm (L x W) feather stitch.

★ Pet leads: use a 3mm triple straight stitch or embroider by hand (*see Hand Embroidery*). Use the diagram in step 3 as a guide for positioning the leads.

5. Place the prepared gusset strips right sides together and stitch the right-hand short side using a ⅜in (1cm) seam allowance. Press the seam open. Fuse the remaining flower unit in the space between the gnomes and appliqué it in place. Sew the remaining ends of the gusset strip together. Press the seam open.

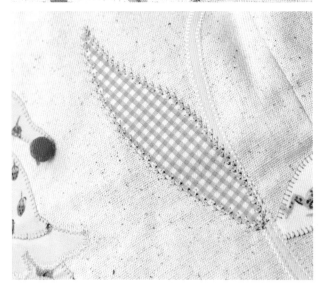

6. To create the base of the cushion, fold the Osnaburg circle in half and press to crease the centre. Place double-sided tape on the wrong side of the zipper, directly behind the teeth (yes, on the back of the teeth). Peel the paper backing off the tape and stick the zipper over the centre crease. Use a decorative stitch on your sewing machine – I used a 3 x 3mm triple blanket stitch. Sew down each edge of the zipper. With small, round-tipped scissors, carefully cut between the two rows of decorative stitches from behind the zipper teeth. Remove this piece of fabric and the double-sided tape. Attach the zipper pull and slide it into the centre of the zipper. Trim off any excess zipper.

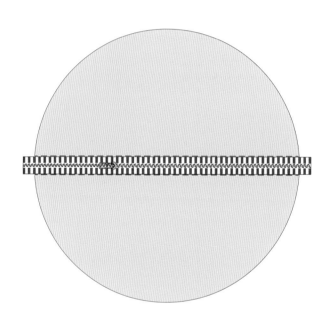

No time for a zipper? You can leave a hole in the gusset to turn the right way out and then hand sew closed once filled.

7. Fold the gusset in quarters and press the edges to crease. Fold the top and base circles in quarters and press towards the edges to crease (alternatively you can measure and mark).

8. Place the top circle right side up with the gusset right side down on top, matching the centre markings of the gusset with the centre markings on the circle. Ease the gusset round the circle, pinning it in position as you go.

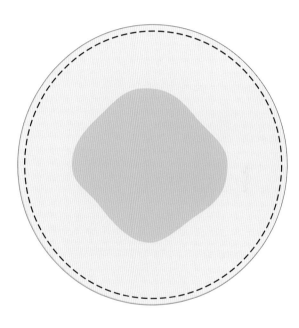

9. Stitch around the circle with a ⅜in (1cm) seam allowance, backstitching at the start and end to reinforce the seam.

10. Ensure the zipper is open a few inches for turning through later. Lay the base circle right side down on top of the other edge of the gusset, matching the centre markings. Pin together, then stitch around the circle with a ⅜in (1cm) seam allowance , again backstitching at the start and end to reinforce the seam. Turn the right way out and fill. If you are using polystyrene beans, you may like to make a separate concealed lining or stitch the zipper closed for safety.

Glue the mini pompoms to the ends of the gnome hats and enjoy chillin' out with your gnomies on your new floor cushion!

Alpaca My Bag!

Calming, sweet natured and social creatures, alpacas just want to make us happy. What better animal to have by your side for your next adventure? This bag is enjoyable and achievable for all skill levels; it even features the easiest zipper installation EVER!

You will need

- **Machine feet:** Regular sewing foot, open toe foot and ¼in foot
- 12 x 15in (30 x 38cm) cork fabric, leather or leather equivalent
- 12in (30cm) square, iron-on fusible web
- 12in (30cm) continuous zipper
- 12in (30cm) square, natural fabric, for outline
- Four 6in (15cm) squares, teal, floral, peach and pink fabrics, for body, chest, head and face
- Five 5in (13cm) squares, mint, citron, lime and brown fabrics, for ears, lips and chin
- Three 4in (10cm) squares, mint, hot pink and rust wool felt, for hair, cheeks and eyelashes
- Three 2in (5cm) squares, blue, black and navy fabrics, for eyes and nose

- 1–2 yds (1–2m) macramé cord or equivalent, ¼in (6mm) wide, for strap
- Sewing thread to match cork fabric
- Contrasting thread, for applying zipper
- Co-ordinating embroidery threads to match appliqué
- 5in (13cm) piece of tassel trim, for alpaca neck
- Peach and red stranded embroidery thread (floss) (optional)
- Large tassels for zipper pull (optional)
- Double-sided tape, ¼in (6mm) wide
- Round-tipped scissors
- Appliqué mat
- Quilting clips

Finished size (excluding strap): 10½ x 12½in (27 x 32cm)

CUTTING INSTRUCTIONS

Cork Fabric

Cut two rectangles, 11 x 14½in (28 x 37cm).

Cut two strips, 1½ x 2½in (4 x 6.5cm), for the strap connectors.

This bag is unlined, so it needs a bit of 'body' – hence the choice of cork fabric for the main material.

Choose a decorative stitch that doesn't go back on itself too much, so that you eliminate drag on the cork fabric. Ensure the middle position of the presser foot is aligned along the edge of the zipper tape. Essentially you are appliquéing the zipper!

CONSTRUCTION

1. Place double-sided tape on the wrong side of the zipper, directly behind the teeth (yes, on the back of the teeth). With a quilting ruler, measure 1½in (4cm) down from the top edge of one cork fabric rectangle. Remove the paper backing from the double-sided tape and position the zipper in place, butting the edge of the zipper up against the ruler.

3. Turn the cork fabric over and use small, round-tipped scissors to carefully cut between the two rows of decorative stitches from behind the zipper teeth. Remove this piece of cork fabric and the double-sided tape. Attach the zipper pull and slide it into the centre of the zipper. Trim off any excess zipper.

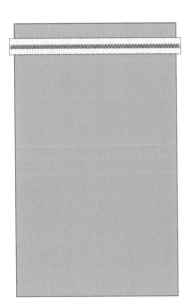

2. Select a decorative stitch and a contrasting thread and use your open toe machine foot to stitch down each side of the zipper tape.

4. Refer to *Modern Appliqué Techniques* at the beginning of this book and use the placement template provided to select your fabrics. Cut them out using the Alpaca My Bag reversed appliqué pieces and the table here.

1	outline	natural fabric
2	body	teal fabric
3	chest	floral fabric
4, 6	ears	mint fabric
5, 7, 21	inner ears & upper lip	citron fabric
8	head	peach fabric
9, 10	cheeks	hot pink felt
11	chin	brown fabric
12	face	pink fabric
13	hair	mint felt
20	lower lip	lime fabric
22	nose	navy fabric
14, 15	lashes	rust felt
16, 17	eyes	blue fabric
18, 19	pupils	black fabric

5. Use the *Layered Appliqué* instructions to construct the units of the alpaca following the number order shown. Use shapes 11–15 for the face unit, shapes 20–22 for the snout and shapes 16–19 for the eyes.

6. Once you have prepared these units, fuse the alpaca together on the appliqué mat, starting from shape number 2 and building the units up until you reach shape number 22. This is now referred to as the alpaca unit. Once cool, remove the appliqué from the mat in one piece. Then place it on top of the outline piece, shape number 1.

7. Position the completed alpaca unit on the prepared cork fabric piece 1½in (4cm) from the base. Fuse it in place with the tip of the iron, but avoid applying too much heat directly to the cork.

8. It's time to sew! Check out *Oh So Glam Decorative Stitches* at the beginning of this book. Now when it comes to selecting stitches for this appliqué, it is important to keep in mind the cork fabric. Avoid tight satin stitches that may perforate the cork too much and result in a hole (*see Appliqué on Cork and Vinyl*). Refer to the list below as a guide for your stitch selection.

★ Body: use a 2 x 5mm (length x width) feather stitch.

★ Head: use a 'furry'-look stitch, grass stitch or zigzag with approximately 4mm stitch width.

★ Ears: use a 4 x 4mm flower stitch.

★ Chest, face, chin, nose, lips, hair, cheeks and inner ears: use a 2 x 2mm blanket stitch.

★ Eyelashes: use a 1.5 x 1.5mm blanket stitch or simple straight stitch (felt doesn't fray).

★ Highlight for eyes: use a 5 x 5mm flower stitch.

9. Pin the tassel trim as shown on the appliqué placement template and stitch it in place.

10. This fancy embroidery (*see Hand Embroidery*) is worth the effort, but if it's not your thing, skip to the next step!

★ Freckles: using three strands of peach stranded embroidery thread (floss), make a French knot (with three wraps of the needle) for a total of six freckles, three on each side of the nose.

★ Tongue: using three strands of red stranded embroidery thread (floss), satin stitch a cute little mouth.

11. Let's construct this woolly cutie! Prepare the strap connectors by placing double-sided tape on the wrong side along each long edge of each piece. Peel off the backing paper and fold the raw edges in to meet in the centre on the wrong side. Sew two lines of stitching along each long side of the strap connectors to strengthen.

12. Fold the strap connectors in half (wrong side together), match up the raw edges and position on the right side of the cork fabric, 1in (2.5cm) down from the top edge.

13. Ensure the zipper is open a couple of inches in the centre. Place both cork fabric pieces, right sides together and use quilting clips to hold in place. Sew around the entire rectangle with a ½in (1cm) seam allowance, backstitching over the zipper and strap connectors to reinforce these areas.

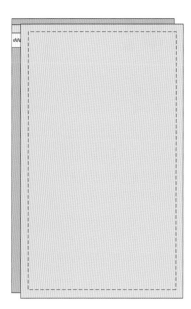

14. To box the corners and create a base for the bag, pinch the bottom corners so that the side seam and base seam align vertically and create a triangle. Measure 1in (2.5cm) from the point, mark and stitch horizontally across the triangle. Cut off the triangle ¼in (6mm) from the stitching line to reduce bulk.

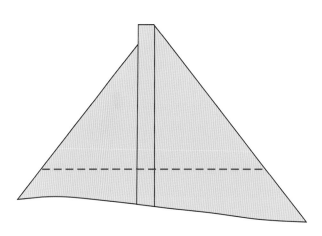

15. Trim the seams, including the strap connector seam allowance to reduce bulk. Turn the bag the right way out through the zipper and topstitch (see Quilting and Finishing Techniques) along the top edge with a ⅜in (1cm) seam allowance. Thread the cord for the bag strap through the strap connectors, cut to the desired length and knot at each end. Fray the ends of the cord for a boho vibe. Add a tassel to the zipper pull!

You're ready for an adventure with your new fabulous make!

Life's Short, Eat Donuts!

I donut about you, but hole-y moley dachshunds are ADORABLE. A dachshund with a donut hula hoop is just too delightful, especially with colourful sprinkles! Rock this apron in the kitchen or while crafting; either way, no one will be able to dull your sparkle.

You will need

- **Machine feet:** Open toe foot and regular sewing foot
- 27 x 44in (70 x 112cm) feature fabric, for apron front
- 27 x 44in (70 x 112cm) lining, for apron back
- 27 x 44in (70 x 112cm) medium-weight woven fusible interfacing
- 27 x 17in (70 x 43cm) fusible web
- 18 x 22in (45 x 56cm) (a fat quarter) cream fabric, for outline around dachshund
- Two 4 x 12in (10 x 30cm) rectangles, blue and mint fabric, for back and belly
- 8in (20 cm) square, sprinkle vinyl, for icing
- 8in (20 cm) square, mustard fabric, for donut
- Three 5in (13in) squares, lime, teal, lilac and mint, for top head, lower head, ears and front foreleg
- Five 2in (5cm) squares, blue, white, mustard, black and lilac, for brows, eyes and tail

- Six 3in (7.5cm) squares, navy, blue, red, pink, green and lime, for snout, mouth, tongue, inner tongue, chin, hind leg and back foreleg
- 1yd (1m) cotton tassel trim
- Four ½in (12.5mm) grommets plus installation tool
- 3¾yd (3.4m) cotton twill tape, 1in (25mm) wide
- Sewing thread to matching apron fabric, plus bobbin thread to match apron back
- Co-ordinating embroidery threads to match appliqué
- Fray stop
- Appliqué mat
- Quilting clips
- Turning tool or chopstick
- Rotary hole cutter

Finished size: 26 x 30in (66 x 76cm)

If you don't have sprinkle vinyl, donut worry! Use a sprinkle, star or confetti printed fabric instead.

D1, 21, 25	donut & eyes	mustard fabric
D2	icing	sprinkle vinyl
1	outline	cream fabric
2, 16, 17	tail & ears	lilac fabric
3, 8	hind leg & top head	lime fabric
4, 9	back foreleg & chin	green fabric
5, 7	belly & front foreleg	mint fabric
6, 10, 18, 19	back, mouth & brows	blue fabric
11	tongue	red fabric
12	inner tongue	pink fabric
13	lower head	teal fabric
14	snout	navy fabric
15	nose	citron fabric
20, 23, 24, 27	eye lid & eye highlight	white fabric
22, 26	pupils	black fabric

CUTTING INSTRUCTIONS

Feature fabric, lining & interfacing

Cut a 27 x 31in (70 x 75cm) rectangle of feature fabric, lining and medium-weight fusible woven interfacing. Fold each fabric in half lengthways so that you have a rectangle 13½ x 31in (35 x 75cm). Position the apron pattern piece provided on the folded feature fabric. Align the straight long edge of the pattern piece with the longest raw edge of the fabric. Cut around the pattern piece and unfold the fabric. Voilà, you have the start of an apron! Repeat for the lining and interfacing rectangles.

With the wrong side of your feature fabric facing up, place the glue side of the woven interfacing down and fuse together.

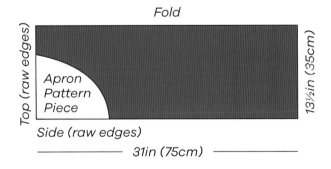

Fold

Top (raw edges)

Apron Pattern Piece

Side (raw edges)

13½in (35cm)

31in (75cm)

CONSTRUCTION

1. Refer to *Modern Appliqué Techniques* at the beginning of this book and use the placement template provided to select your fabrics. Cut them out using the Life's Short, Eat Donuts reversed appliqué pieces and the table here.

During the fusible appliqué process, please be mindful when working with heat-sensitive materials like sprinkle vinyl. Often products such as vinyl, which have a fabric backing, can be ironed gently from the back, but you should NEVER iron them from the right side. Always test your product first before diving into your project. You donut want to melt your work!

2. Use the *Layered Appliqué* instructions to construct units of the dachshund and donut by following the number order below. Use shapes 9–15 for the snout unit and shapes 20–27 for the eyes. Use a glue stick to build the donut unit D1–D2.

3. Once you have prepared the above units, fuse them together on the appliqué mat, starting from shape number 2 (excluding the outline) and building the units up until you reach shape number 27 (leave the donut unit off). This is now referred to as the dachshund unit. Once cool, remove the appliqué from the mat in one piece.

4. Slide the dachshund unit through the hole in the donut so that the legs are partially hidden. Refer to the appliqué placement template as a guide.

5. Position shape number 1 (the outline) on the front of the apron in the centre and 2in (5cm) down from the top edge and fuse in place. Centre the prepared dachshund unit inside the outline and fuse it in place. Remember to avoid ironing the sprinkle vinyl on the donut as it is heat sensitive.

6. Oh, donut ever doubt yourself... it's time to stitch! It is important to keep in mind the vinyl elements of this appliqué. The sprinkle vinyl isn't sticky so there is no need for a non-stick foot. However, I suggest keeping the stitching fairly simple for this element.

★ Icing: use a 2.5 x 2.5mm blanket stitch.

★ Outline, donut, legs, tail, tongue, mouth, chin, head, snout and nose: use a 2 x 2mm blanket stitch.

★ Eyes: use a 1.5 x 1.5mm blanket stitch.

★ Highlight in eyes: use a 5 x 5mm star stitch, one star in the centre of each white circle.

★ Ears: use a 4mm stem stitch.

★ Back: use a 'furry'-look stitch, grass stitch or zigzag with approximately 6mm stitch width.

★ Belly: use a 5 x 5mm star stitch.

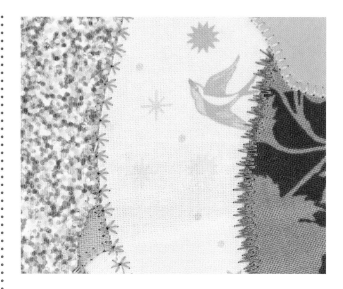

7. Lay the apron right side up and position the tassel trim along the bottom edge. Align the raw edge of the fabric with the tassel tape (the tassels will face towards the top of the apron). Tack (baste) in place.

8. Place the two apron pieces right sides together and pin. Ensure the tassels are all tucked in between the layers. Using a 2.5mm straight stitch, sew the apron pieces together with a ⅜in (1cm) seam allowance, leaving a 5in (13cm) gap in one side.

9. Turn the apron the right way out through the gap, pushing the corners out nicely with a turning tool or chopstick. Fold in the seam allowance where the gap was left and give everything a good press with an iron (remember not to press the sprinkle vinyl). Insert a couple of pins to hold the edges of the gap together.

10. With a 3mm straight stitch and a ⅛in (3mm) seam allowance, topstitch around the entire apron (see *Quilting and Finishing Techniques*).

11. Measure 1in (2.5cm) down from the top corner and 1in (2.5cm) in from the sides of the 'bib' section of the apron and mark for the grommet placement. Use a hole cutter and remove the circle where marked. Place some fray stop around the edge of the holes and insert grommets as per the manufacturer's directions included with the installation tool. Repeat this for the side grommets.

12. Cut the twill tape for the straps, two pieces 39in (1m) and two 27½in (70cm). Add some fray stop at each end.

13. Feed the longer straps through the side grommets and the shorter straps through the top bib section. Fold the end closest to the grommet over by ½in (1cm) and then fold an additional 2in (5cm) up and hold in place with a pin. Stitch a small rectangle around the folded ½in (1cm) section to secure. Fold the other end of the strap over by ¼in (6mm) and then again to enclose. Sew a line of stitching to secure and repeat this step for all straps.

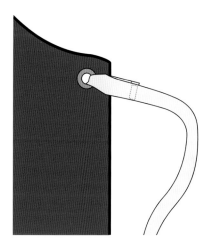

Give yourself a big round of ap-paws – you're going to look dashing in this apron!

Let's Flamingle!

Whether it's a day at the beach with the chicks or a night out with the girls, you'll be ready to flamingle with this rad bag! Featuring gorgeous Liberty fabrics and raffia, I know you'll be tickled pink when you create this beauty. Sew it like the flock star you are!

You will need

- **Machine feet:** regular sewing foot, open toe foot and ¼in foot
- 20 x 44in (50 x 112cm) cream raffia fabric
- 1yd x 44in (100 x 112cm) natural colour cotton fabric
- 20 x 17in (50 x 43cm) fusible web
- 20 x 40in (50 x 100cm) tracing paper
- 30in x 44in (70 x 112cm) fusible stabilizer
- 30 x 44in (70 x 112cm) medium-weight woven fusible interfacing
- Five 10in (25cm) squares, pink, red, mustard, citron and black cotton fabrics, for heads and necks, cheeks, beaks, eyes and beak tip details
- Two 10in (25cm) squares, Liberty fabric in shades of pink and red, for flamingo bellies

- Two 5in (13cm) squares, blue and teal cotton fabrics, for inner beaks
- Two 3in (8cm) squares, Liberty fabric in shades of blue and teal, for floral beaks
- Two 2in (5cm) squares, white and navy cotton fabrics, for nose highlights and pupils
- Leather straps or pre-made handles plus rivets to attach (optional)
- Cream sewing thread, plus matching bobbin
- Co-ordinating embroidery threads to match appliqué
- Appliqué mat
- Quilting clips

Finished size (excluding handles): 18in (46cm)

CUTTING INSTRUCTIONS

Raffia fabric

Trace the 17in (43cm) diameter circle on the appliqué placement template provided onto tracing paper and cut out. Pin onto the raffia fabric and cut two.

Natural colour cotton fabric

Trace the 14¾in (37.5cm) diameter circle on the placement template onto tracing paper and cut out. Fold the fabric in half, pin the template to the fabric and cut two circles. Repeat so that you have two pairs. Cut two 5 x 34in (13 x 86cm) strips.

Fusible stabilizer

Cut two 14¾in (37.5cm) circles using the smaller paper template again. Cut a 5 x 34in (13 x 86cm) rectangle.

Medium-weight woven fusible interfacing

Cut two 14¾in (37.5cm) circles using the smaller paper template again. Cut a 5 x 34in (13 x 86cm) rectangle.

Liberty fabric

Liberty fabric is made from 100% cotton and is delightfully fine, soft and durable. During the fusible appliqué process, Liberty fabric needs to be treated differently to regular fabric to prevent it from becoming transparent. You need to iron the fusible woven interfacing onto the wrong side of the Liberty fabric PRIOR to ironing the fusible web shapes.

CONSTRUCTION

1. Refer to *Modern Appliqué Techniques* at the beginning of this book and use the placement template provided to select your fabrics. Cut them out using the Let's Flamingle reversed appliqué pieces and the table below.

L1, R3	flamingo body & cheek	pink fabric
L3, R1	cheek & flamingo body	red fabric
L2, R2	flamingo belly	pink/red Liberty fabric
L10, R4	eye & beak	mustard fabric
L4, R10	beak & eye	citron fabric
L5, R5	inner beak	teal/blue fabric
L6, R6	floral beak	blue/teal Liberty fabric
L7, L8, R7, R8	beak tip detail	black fabric
L9, R9	nose highlight	white fabric
L11, R11	pupils	navy fabric

2. Use the *Layered Appliqué* instructions to construct units of the flamingo beak and eyes by following the number order here. Use shapes L5–L9 for the left inner beak unit, shapes R5–R9 for the right inner beak unit, shapes L10–L11 for the left eye and shapes R10–R11 for the right eye.

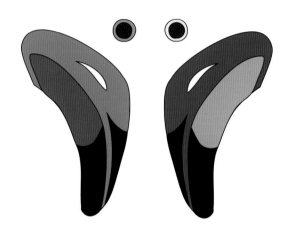

3. Next, construct the rest of the flamingo heads following the order here. Use shapes L1–L4 for the left flamingo and shapes R1–R4 for the right flamingo. Then apply the beak and eye units from step 2. Once you have prepared the above units, fuse them together on the appliqué mat and peel each flamingo off in one complete unit.

4. Position the 14in (35.5cm) pattern piece in the centre of one of the raffia circles and pin it in place. Using a 2.5mm straight stitch, sew around the edge of the paper template in a similar-coloured thread. This line of stitching will be a placement guide. Unpin and remove the paper template. Repeat this step for the remaining raffia circle.

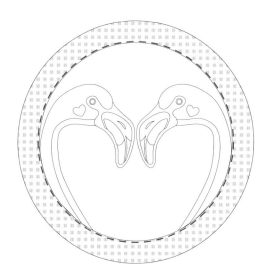

5. Place both flamingo units on one of the raffia circles as per the placement template, keeping within the stitching guideline sewn in step 4. Carefully fuse the applique to the raffia for five seconds or until the flamingo units are attached.

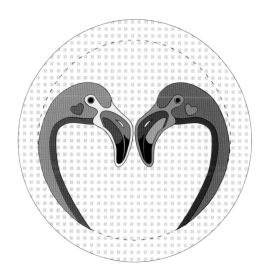

6. It's time to sew, babe! Now when it comes to selecting stitches for this appliqué it is important to keep in mind the open weave of the raffia fabric. Use a large, simple stitch that will not get lost in the weave. Refer to the list below as a guide for your stitch selection.

★ Neck & outer beak: use a 3 x 3mm triple blanket stitch.

★ Inner neck (Liberty fabric): use a 4 x 4mm flower stitch.

★ Heart cheeks and inner beak pieces: use a 2 x 2mm triple blanket stitch.

★ Eyes and beak highlight: use a 1.5 x 1.5mm blanket stitch.

Oh flock! You don't have raffia fabric? No need to get in a pickle, you can substitute other open-weave fabrics. Just pick something with a nice amount of body, otherwise your bag may be a little floppy!

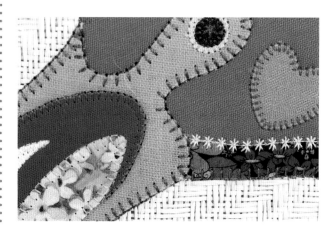

7. Fuse the stabilizer to the wrong side of two fabric circles and one of the rectangles. Fuse the woven interfacing pieces to the wrong side of the remaining two fabric circles and rectangle.

8. Place one of each of the prepared circles right sides together (one with the stabilizer together with one with the woven interfacing) and do the same for the two rectangles. Pin and sew around these pieces with a ⅜in (1cm) seam allowance, leaving a gap of about 3in (7.5cm) in the seam on the circles and 5in (13cm) in one long edge of the rectangle for turning.

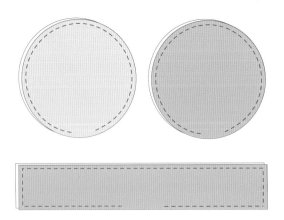

9. Carefully clip the curves within the seam allowance of the circles and the corners of the rectangle and turn the right way out. Roll the seam between your fingers so that it lies flat and ensure the corners of the rectangle are fully pushed out. Fold in the raw edges of fabric where the gaps were left and press with an iron. Use pins to hold the seam in place.

10. Turn over the raffia circles so that the wrong sides are facing up. Place one of the prepared fabric circles (stabilizer side facing up) in the centre of each raffia circle. Pin to hold the layers together.

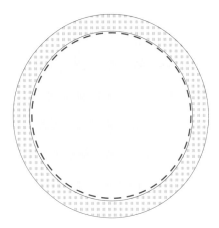

11. Using cream thread and matching bobbin, topstitch round the fabric circles with a ⅛in (3mm) seam allowance (see Quilting and Finishing Techniques). The raffia is face down on your machine bed, so it's important to have matching bobbin thread.

12. Topstitch along the short edges of the rectangle. Then fold in half lengthwise and mark the centre point on each long edge. This will serve as a guide for positioning the gusset.

13. Mark the centre base edge of the fabric circles, paying particular attention to the side with the flamingos. Fold and match the flamingo heads together and place a small mark on the fabric side to guide with placement.

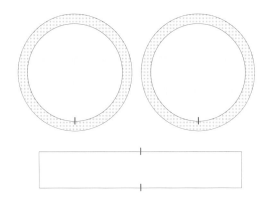

14. Place the appliquéd circle raffia side down. Matching the centre mark on the rectangle with the centre base mark on the circle, pin the rectangle around the circle, easing it into position as you go.

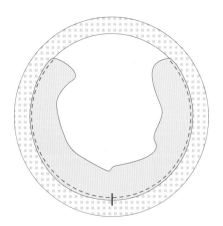

15. Topstitch the rectangle in place with a ⅛in (3mm) seam allowance, backstitching at the start and end of the rectangle to reinforce the seams.

16. Place the remaining circle raffia side down on the other edge of the gusset, lining up the centre base mark with the remaining centre mark on the rectangle. Using quilting clips to hold the previous raffia circle out of the way, pin the rectangle around the remaining circle. Topstitch and reinforce the stitching at the start and end by stitching backwards and forwards a couple of times.

17. Position straps at your desired length, approximately 2in (5cm) down from the top fabric circle. Attach straps either by hand sewing, machine (if your straps are machine sew-able) or with rivets. You can also use belts for straps or add one long strap either side of the gusset (see tip below).

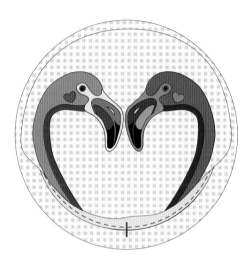

18. Carefully pull apart the weave along the edges of the raffia to create a fringed effect. It will not unravel further than the stitching line. Give it a trim and you are ready to rock it!

Place pins horizontally when pinning the rectangle to the circle, as this will make it easier to sew.

Take it up a feather... Add a pocket or magnetic clasp for an extra design element! Give it some length and add a long strap from each side of the gusset.

Stand out from the flock with your gorgeous one-of-a-kind make!

Be-leaf in You

If you just can't get enough of anything plant related, you'll be in full bloom when you create this gorgeous textile hanging plant. Even a serial plant killer can keep this beauty alive. If you can't find metallic rope, don't sweat it: just use a cotton or natural option – it will still look unbe-leaf-able!

You will need

- **Machine feet:** Open toe foot, Teflon foot and ¼in foot
- 18 x 22in (46 x 56cm) citron linen fabric, for background
- 18 x 22in (46 x 56cm) natural-coloured fabric, for lining and pot
- 20 x 22in (50 x 56cm) medium-weight woven fusible interfacing
- 12 x 17in (30 x 43cm) fusible web
- 14 x 22in (35 x 56cm) bag wadding (batting)
- 6 x 22in (15 x 56cm) transparent vinyl, for hanger
- 8in (20cm) square, red glitter vinyl, for rainbow and tassel
- 6in (15cm) square, pink glitter vinyl, for tassel
- Two 5in (13cm) squares, hot pink and light pink fabric, for rainbow

- Two 5in (13cm) squares, mustard and rust wool felt, for stems
- 2in (5cm) square, printed fabric, for heart
- About 35 fabric scraps, 2 x 5in (5 x 13cm) each, for improv leaves
- Pink stranded embroidery thread (floss)
- 32in (80cm) metallic rope
- 17in (43cm) wooden dowel, 1in (25mm) diameter
- Appliqué mat
- Glue stick (optional)
- Rotary cutter, quilting ruler and cutting mat
- Quilting clips
- Craft glue, for tassels

Finished size (excluding hanger): 13 x 16in (33 x 40.5cm)

CUTTING INSTRUCTIONS

Linen fabric and medium-weight woven fusible interfacing

Cut one 17 x 19in (43 x 48.5cm) rectangle of each, then fuse the interfacing to the wrong side of the linen.

Bag wadding (batting)

Cut one 13 x 16in (33 x 40.5cm) rectangle.

Lining

Cut one 12¾ x 15¾in (32.5 x 40cm) rectangle.

Transparent vinyl

Cut two 5 x 6in (13 x 15cm) rectangles.

Glitter vinyls (pink and red)

Cut one 3 x 6in (7.5 x 15cm) rectangle of each colour.

Cut one ½ x 3in (1 x 7.5cm) rectangle of each colour.

CONSTRUCTION

1. Improv quilting: Place two scrap fabric rectangles right sides together. Although it's tempting to keep the edges aligned, they look more effective placed at different angles. Sew them together with a ¼in (6mm) seam allowance (1a). Trim off the excess fabric (1b). Press the seam to one side (1c), add the next rectangle (1d) and trim off the excess seam allowance. Keep in mind the size of the finished leaf: each one will need 5–7 rectangles (1e). Press firmly, particularly the seams (1f).

2. Refer to *Modern Appliqué Techniques* at the beginning of this book and use the placement template provided to select your fabrics. Cut them out using the Be-leaf in You reversed appliqué pieces and the table below.

5, 7, 8, 9, 10	leaves	prepared improv fabric
1, 2, 3	stems	rust wool felt
6	stem	mustard wool felt
4	pot	natural fabric
11	large rainbow	red glitter vinyl
12	middle rainbow	hot pink fabric
13	small rainbow	light pink fabric
14	heart	patterned fabric

3. Use the *Layered Appliqué* instructions to construct units of the hanging plant by following the number order here. Use shapes 11–13 for the rainbow unit. Do not heat glitter vinyl; fuse carefully around it (*see Appliqué on Cork and Vinyl*), then add it to shape 4 (pot), along with shape 14. Use a glue stick if needed to hold the rainbow in place.

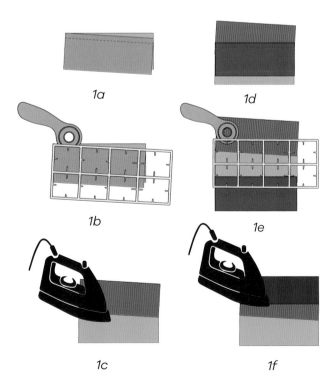

1a

1d

1b

1e

1c

1f

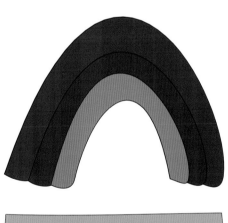

4. Fuse the prepared units together on the appliqué mat, starting from shape 1 and working up to shape 14.

5. Lay the prepared linen fabric right side down and position the bag wadding (batting) on top. Measure to check it's central – important for a later step – and use basting spray or pins to hold it in place.

6. Let's grow! It's time to quilt. Add interest to the linen background with some modern quilting (see Quilting and Finishing Techniques). If you'd like to achieve the same quilting, follow the measurements below. Ensure you stitch almost to the edge of the fabric.

★ First quilt lines vertically ¾in (2cm) apart (6a).

★ Then quilt lines horizontally 1½in (4cm) apart (6b).

★ This creates a grid of quilting (6c).

★ Alternate colours and make two lines of stitching intersecting each horizontal line as shown (6d).

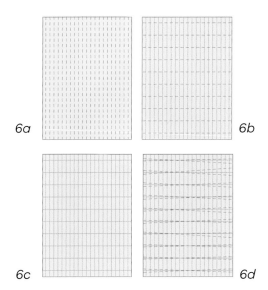

6a 6b
6c 6d

7. Place the quilted unit on a cutting mat and position a quilting ruler at a 45-degree angle along the edge of the linen fabric and ¼in (6mm) out from a corner of the bag wadding (batting). Use a rotary cutter to remove this piece (6). Repeat on the remaining corners.

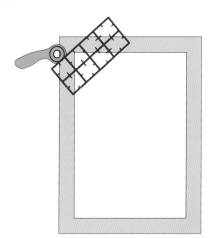

8. Lay this unit on an ironing surface (8a) and fold the exposed sides of the fabric in half towards the edge of the bag wadding (batting), then press to crease (8b). Fold the entire unit in half almost diagonally as you pinch a corner together along the 45-degree angle you created (right sides together). Sew along the line formed (8c) to create a mitred corner. Repeat for each side. Trim the seam allowance and turn towards the back so that it lies flat over the bag wadding (batting). Press and hold with some quilting clips. This will be referred to as 'facing'.

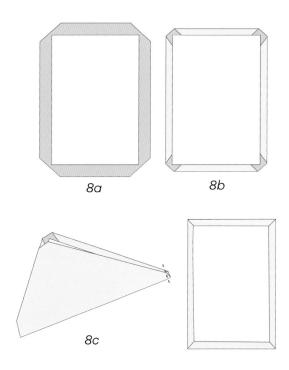

8a 8b
8c

9. With the quilted background in a portrait orientation, position the prepared appliqué unit ¾in (2cm) from the base and fuse in place. Remember to avoid any vinyl elements with the iron. The leaves may take a little longer to fuse due to the thickness of the seams. Apply a small amount of fray stop to any sections of the leaves that didn't end up with fusible web or that have fluffy sections.

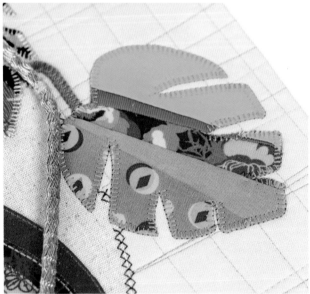

10. Keep growing! You're ready to stitch the appliqué. It is important to keep in mind the vinyl elements of this appliqué. I highly recommend using a Teflon-coated (non-stick) foot for areas where the foot will be touching vinyl. Otherwise, your regular foot may stick and grip to the vinyl, causing your sewing machine to stitch inconsistently. I'd also suggest keeping the stitching fairly simple for these elements.

★ Stems: use a 5 x 1.3mm (W x L) triple zigzag. Sew a row of stitching through the middle of each stem.

★ Leaves: use a 3 x 2mm (W x L) triple blanket stitch.

★ Rainbow: use a 3mm triple straight stitch.

★ Heart: use a 2 x 2mm blanket stitch.

★ Pot: use a 4 x 4mm cross stitch.

11. Turn your textile art over, remove any quilting clips and insert the lining piece. Tuck the lining under the prepared mitred corners. Make sure that it is lying flat and reattach the quilting clips. Hand sew the facing to the lining to secure. You could machine sew this, but you will end up with additional lines of stitching on the front.

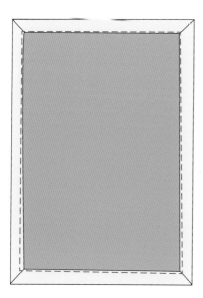

12. Fold the two transparent vinyl pieces in half so that they are 5 x 3in (13 x 7.5cm). Position the long raw edges of the vinyl ⅝in (1.5cm) down from the top and ¼in (6mm) in from each side. Use quilting clips to hold them. Topstitch with a ¼in (6mm) seam allowance along the top edge to hold the vinyl in place.

13. Fold the rope in half and use a lark's head knot to attach it around the middle of the dowel. The two lengths of rope create the illusion that the pot is hanging. Position the rope on either side of the plant, about ¼in (6mm) down from the top edge of the pot. With a large sewing needle and stranded embroidery thread (floss), push the needle slightly through the top layers of fabric and sew a few wraps around the rope to secure at each side. Knot the stranded embroidery thread (floss), bury the threads in the layers of fabric and trim to hide them.

14. Repeat step 13 to secure the rope in place at the top. Bring the two strands of rope together at the bottom and secure with stranded embroidery thread (floss). Leave one rope hanging an additional 2in (5cm) and the other 4in (10cm) past the embroidery wrap. Place tape around the rope prior to cutting to prevent fraying.

15. Prepare the tassels by laying the 3 x 6in (7.5 x 15cm) glitter vinyl rectangles wrong side up. Mark 1in (2.5cm) in along the short edge, for the tops of the tassels. Measure every ⅛in (3mm) along the long edge, but only up mark to the 1in (2.5cm) mark – the fringe will be 2in (5cm) long. Use scissors to cut along each ⅛in (3mm) marking, but leave the 1in (2.5cm) section uncut! Apply glue along the uncut section and position the end of the rope at the start of the 1in (2.5cm) section. Roll the tassel around the end of the rope as tightly as you can. Apply glue to the ½ x 3in (1 x 7.5cm) strips and wrap each one around the centre of the tassel in the opposite colour, then trim any excess. Tie stranded embroidery thread (floss) around the strip and wrap around tightly for both security and style!

Your plant-loving friends are going to DIG your new textile wall art!

Toucan Do It!

Any colour lover will adore this toucan clutch. I mean, this feathered creature is already iconic for its exotic and tropical vibes, which are only further enhanced with a fruit salad headpiece. Just don't expect to blend in if you're carrying this rainbow creation!

You will need

- **Machine feet:** Open toe foot, zipper foot and regular sewing foot
- 12 x 22in (30 x 56cm) brown raffia fabric
- 12 x 22in (30 x 56cm) lining fabric
- 12 x 44in (30 x 112cm) medium-weight woven fusible interfacing
- 12 x 44in (30 x 112cm) fusible fleece
- 16 x 17in (40.5 x 43cm) iron-on fusible web
- 12in (30cm) square, natural fabric, for outline
- Four 6in (15cm) squares, black, blue, citron and lilac fabrics, for body, beak, chest and scarf
- Ten 3in (7.5cm) squares, orange, red, green, yellow, magenta, rust, pink, mint, lilac and tangerine fabrics, for pineapple, melon, pineapple top, banana, apple and beak features

- Three 2in (5cm) squares, mint, blue and white fabrics, for eyes and spots
- 12in (30cm) zipper
- Three mini buttons or sequins, for melon seeds
- 1yd (1m) piece of raffia fringe trim
- Co-ordinating embroidery threads to match appliqué
- Jumbo pompom
- Washi tape (optional)
- Appliqué mat
- Quilting clips

Finished size: 10 x 12½in (25 x 32cm)

CUTTING INSTRUCTIONS

Raffia fabric, lining fabric, medium-weight woven fusible interfacing and fusible fleece

Cut two rectangles, 10 x 12in (25 x 30cm) of each. Fuse the medium-weight woven fusible interfacing to the wrong side of the lining fabric rectangles, followed by the fusible fleece. With the pieces laid landscape, pin the curved base pattern piece provided in the bottom left and right corners of both raffia and lining pieces and trim away from each rectangle. If the raffia fabric is fraying, place some washi tape around the edges.

If you have a selection of little scraps of fabric in the right colour, you can use them rather than trying to find a whole 6in (15cm), 3in (7.5cm) or 2in (5cm) square of a single fabric. For example, I've used several different lilac fabrics for my toucan's fabulous headscarf.

CONSTRUCTION

1. Refer to *Modern Appliqué Techniques* at the beginning of this book and use the placement template provided to select your fabrics. Cut them out using the Toucan Do It! reversed appliqué pieces and the table here.

1	outline	natural fabric
2, 3	banana ends	black fabric
4	banana	yellow fabric
5, 8, 10	pineapple top, apple leaf & melon rind	green fabrics
6	pineapple	orange fabric
7	apple	magenta fabric
9	melon	red fabric
11, 12, 13, 14	scarf	lilac fabrics
15, 22	body & pupil	black fabric
16	chest	citron fabric
17	heart	peach fabric
18, 19, 20	spots	blue & purple fabrics
21, 24	eye & beak	blue fabrics
23	highlight	white fabric
25, 26, 27, 28, 29	beak features	rust, pink, mint, lilac & tangerine fabrics

2. Use the *Layered Appliqué* instructions to construct units of the toucan following the number order shown. Use shapes 25–29 for the beak unit, shapes 21–23 for the eye unit, shapes 16–17 for the chest unit and shapes 2–14 for the fruit crown unit.

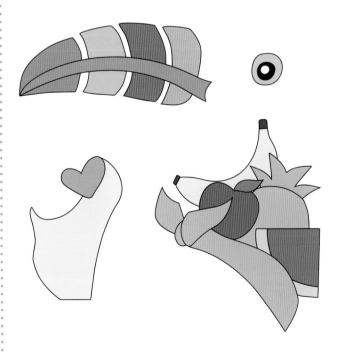

3. Once you have prepared the units, fuse the toucan together on the appliqué mat, starting from shape number 2 and building the units up until you reach shape number 29. This is now referred to as the toucan unit. Once cool, remove the appliqué from the mat in one piece. Then place it on top of the outline piece, shape number 1.

4. Position the toucan in the centre of the raffia and carefully fuse it in place.

5. Fly high, it's time to sew! Give your toucan some texture with fun decorative stitches. Check out *Oh So Glam Decorative Stitches* at the beginning of this book. Contrast some threads with the fabric and make the stitching POP! Use the following as a guide.

★ Body: use a 'furry'-look stitch, grass stitch or zigzag with approximately 4mm stitch width.

★ Chest: use a 3 x 3mm arrowhead decorative stitch, which has a hand-stitched look.

★ Beak: use a 4 x 4mm flower stitch

★ Heart, fruit, scarf and spots: use a 2 x 2mm blanket stitch

★ Eye and pupil: use a 1.5 x 1.5mm blanket stitch

★ Highlight: use a 6 x 6mm star stitch

★ Sew three buttons or sequins on the melon as seeds

6. Attach the raffia fringe to both sides and the base of the bag. Match the raw edges, pin and then tack (baste) in place with a ⅛in (3mm) seam allowance. Use quilting clips to hold the raffia fringe away from seams.

7. Let's add a zipper! Lay the prepared raffia fabric (right side facing up) and place the zipper (wrong side facing up) along the straight edge of the raffia rectangle. Then place a lining rectangle on top (right side facing down). Ensure the edges are matched up and the zipper is sandwiched between the two layers of fabric. Pin in place and then sew together with a ¼in (6mm) seam allowance (you may like to use a zipper foot).

8. Open the seam and press the fabric away from the zipper. Topstitch (see Quilting and Finishing Techniques) with a ¼in (6mm) seam allowance.

9. Using the remaining raffia and lining pieces, repeat steps 7 and 8 on the other side of the zipper.

10. Slide the zipper pull so that there is an opening of approximately 3in (7.5cm), not all the way. Pin the two raffia pieces together with right sides facing and then pin the two lining pieces together with right sides facing. Ensure the zipper faces towards the lining. Sew around the entire unit with a ⅜in (1cm) seam allowance, leaving a 5in (13cm) gap in the base of the lining piece.

11. Clip the seam and any excess zipper. Carefully turn right side out through the gap in the lining and press. Hand or machine stitch the gap in the lining closed. Attach the jumbo pompom to your zipper pull.

Rock your clutch with a colourful and quirky outfit!

You Are Dino-mite!

ROAR!!! Don't worry, they're mostly armless. The T-rex has to be one of the coolest dinosaurs, but have you ever wondered why its arms are so short? It's so that everything it holds is close to its heart! Who knew the T-rex was so sweet?

You will need (for adult size)

- **Machine foot:** Open toe foot
- Garment, denim jacket or similar, for upcycling
- 12 x 17in (30 x 43cm) iron-on fusible web
- 12in (30cm) square, hot pink fabric, for body
- 8in (20cm) square, rust fabric, for back
- Four 4in (10cm) squares, mustard fabrics, for arms
- Three 4in (10cm) squares, patterned fabrics, for flowers
- Two 4in (10cm) squares, white and red fabric, for teeth and tongue
- Seven 2in (5cm) squares, blush, blue, navy, white, lime, black and rust fabrics, for heart, eye, pupil, nostrils and claws
- Stranded embroidery thread (floss) for face features (optional)
- Fringe trim, same length as inner sleeve measurement of garment (optional)
- Appliqué mat

Finished size: 8 x 10½in (20 x 27cm)

MEASURING INSTRUCTIONS

A perfect way to upcycle or repurpose a denim jacket is with a T-riffic appliqué! When you've found your jacket, measure the available appliqué space and check that the finished size will fit. If the appliqué size needs to be adjusted simply increase or decrease the You Are Dino-mite reversed appliqué pieces and the placement template provided. For the kid's jacket shown in the main photo, I shrank the templates down to 80% and mirrored them so that the dinosaurs will face each other when the jackets are worn, if the wearers are side by side.

CONSTRUCTION

1. Refer to *Modern Appliqué Techniques* at the beginning of this book and use the placement template provided to select your fabrics. Cut them out using the You Are Dino-mite! reversed appliqué pieces and the table below.

1, 2, 4, 6, 37, 38, 39	claws	rust fabric
3, 5, 7, 40	arms	mustard fabric
8–10, 12–25	teeth	white fabric
11	tongue	red fabric
26	back	rust fabric
28, 29, 30	flowers	patterned fabric
27	body	hot pink fabric
31	heart	blush fabric
32	eye	blue fabric
33	pupil	navy fabric
34	highlight	white fabric
35	nostril	lime fabric
36	inner nostril	black fabric

2. Use the *Layered Appliqué* instructions to construct units of the T-rex following the number order shown. Use shapes 1–7 for the peace hand unit, shapes 37–40 for the arm unit, shapes 8–11 for the tongue unit, shapes 32–34 for the eye unit, shapes 35–36 for the nostril unit and shapes 26–27 for the body unit.

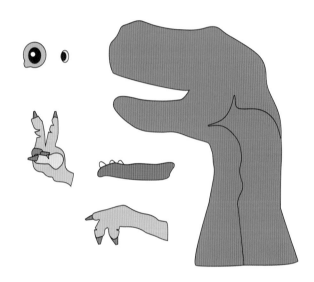

3. Once you have prepared the units, fuse them together on the appliqué mat, starting from shape number 1 and building up until you reach shape number 40. This is now referred to as the dino unit. Once cool, remove the appliqué from the mat in one piece.

4. Position the appliqué on the denim jacket and fuse with an iron for five seconds.

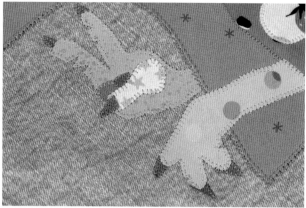

5. ROAR... it means sew! Give your dino some texture with fun decorative stitches. Check out *Oh So Glam Decorative Stitches* at the beginning of this book. Contrast some threads with the fabric and make the stitching POP! Use the following as a guide.

★ Body: use a 2 x 2mm triple blanket stitch (near mouth section and inner body) and a 3 x 3mm arrowhead decorative stitch, which has a hand-stitched look.

★ Back: use a 4 x 4mm cross stitch.

★ Teeth, tongue, claws, nostril, eye, heart, arms and flowers: use a 2 x 2mm blanket stitch.

★ Highlight: use a 6 x 6mm star stitch.

6. Peace out and add some optional hand embroidery (*see Hand Embroidery*). With three strands of stranded embroidery thread (floss) backstitch the eyelashes, brow and dimples as illustrated on the appliqué placement template.

7. Hand sew some fringe trim along the arm seams of the denim jacket or add some rad patches!

Rock your ROAR-SOME denim jacket with your mini DINO-MITE bestie.

Rad & Fab

I'm all about letting the good times roll. Whether you dance on wheels, cruise the beach boardwalk, tackle a roller derby or dive bravely down the skate ramp, you need this rad backpack to hold your essentials. Rock it as a tote, then convert it into a backpack in one swift action.

You will need

- **Machine feet:** Regular sewing foot, open toe foot, ¼in foot and Teflon foot
- 12in (30cm) square, iron-on fusible web
- 15 x 44in (38 x 112cm) fusible fleece
- 30 x 44in (76 x 112cm) medium-weight woven fusible interfacing
- 15 x 44in (38 x 112cm) background fabric
- 15 x 44in (38 x 112cm) lining fabric
- 4 x 44in (10 x 112cm) contrasting fabric, for drawstring enclosure
- 4 x 44in (10 x 112cm) vinyl or leather, for base
- Five 10in (25cm) squares, cream fabric, for shoe
- 8in (20cm) square, cork fabric, leather or fabric, for heel
- 6in (25cm) square, mustard, for tongue
- Five 5in (13cm) squares, red, pink, citron, teal and blue fabrics, for rainbow, inner skate base and sock
- Two 4in (10cm) squares, gold and pink glitter vinyl, for star and heart

- Two 2in (5cm) squares, brown and black fabrics, for toe, inner heel and stopper
- Two 10in (25cm) squares, teal and blue fabrics, for skate base and wheels
- Two 1¼in (30mm) buttons
- 16 eyelets, 4–5mm, plus installation tool
- 1yd (1m) ribbon, ⅜in (1cm) wide, for shoelaces
- 24in (60cm) webbing, 1in (25mm) wide, for handles
- 4–5yd (4-5m) macramé cord or equivalent, ¼in (6mm) wide, for straps
- Two ½in (1.2cm) grommets, plus installation tool
- Cream sewing thread, plus matching bobbin
- Co-ordinating embroidery threads to match appliqué
- Appliqué mat
- Fray stop
- Rotary hole cutter

Finished size (excluding handles): 12 x 16in (30 x 40.5cm)

CUTTING INSTRUCTIONS

Background fabric, medium-weight woven fusible interfacing, and fusible fleece

Cut two 14 x 14in (35.5 x 35.5cm) squares of each. Fuse the interfacing to the wrong side of the background fabric.

Lining fabric and medium-weight fusible interfacing

Cut two 14 x 16in (35.5 x 40.5cm) rectangles of each. Fuse the interfacing to the wrong side of the lining fabric.

Fusible fleece

Cut two 14 x 16½in (35.5 x 42cm) rectangles.

Contrasting fabric and medium-weight woven fusible interfacing

Cut four 1¾ x 11½in (4.5 x 29cm) rectangles of each. Fuse the interfacing to the wrong side of all four rectangles.

Vinyl (base)

Cut two 3 x 14in (7.5 x 35.5cm) rectangles.

During the fusible appliqué process, please be mindful when working with heat-sensitive materials. Often products like glitter vinyl, with a fabric backing, can be ironed gently from the back, but they should NEVER be ironed from the right side. Always test your product first before diving into your project.

CONSTRUCTION

1. Refer to *Modern Appliqué Techniques* at the beginning of this book and use the placement template provided to select your fabrics. Cut them out using the Rad & Fab reversed appliqué pieces and the table here.

3, 5	inner skate base & skate base	teal fabrics
4, 19	inner heel & toe	brown fabrics
6	stopper	black fabric
1, 2, 7, 8, 9	wheels & sock	blue fabrics
10, 12, 14	shoe	cream fabric
13	tongue	mustard fabric
11	heart	pink glitter vinyl
15, 16, 17	rainbow	red, pink & citron fabric
18	star	gold glitter vinyl
20	heel	cork, leather or vinyl fabric

2. Use the *Layered Appliqué* instructions to construct units of the skate following the number order shown. Use a glue pen to secure vinyl elements and iron from the back of the appliqué mat. Use shapes 15–19 for the rainbow unit, shapes 1–8 for the skate base unit and shapes 11–14 for the tongue unit.

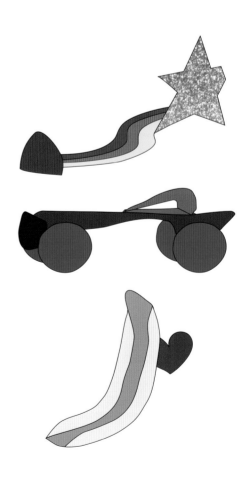

3. Once you have prepared the above units, fuse the skate together on the appliqué mat, starting from shape number 1 and building the units up until you reach shape number 18. Remember not to fuse the glitter vinyl; use a glue stick and be cautious fusing the cork fabric too (*see Appliqué on Cork & Vinyl*). You can carefully flip your appliqué mat over and fuse from the back. This is now referred to as the skate unit. Once cool, remove it from the mat in one piece.

4. Position the skate appliqué on the centre of the prepared background rectangle, approximately 1in (2.5cm) from the base edge, and fuse it in place.

5. It's time to sew, babe! Give your skate extra style with some fun decorative stitches. Check out *Oh So Glam Decorative Stitching* at the beginning of this book. Contrast some threads with the fabric and make the stitching POP! Use the following as a guide.

★ Skate and toe: use a 3 x 3mm triple blanket stitch.

★ Skate lace section: use a 1.5 x 1.5mm triple blanket stitch.

★ Sock: use a 4 x 4mm flower stitch.

★ Heart: use a 4mm satin stitch or blanket stitch.

★ Star, rainbow, tongue, skate base and stopper: use a 2 x 2mm triple blanket stitch.

6. Attach the buttons to the centre of the two facing wheels.

7. This is one cool skate bag – it has 3D laces! You'll find the positioning guides for the eyelets on the appliqué placement template. Make sure the eyelets aren't going to affect any of your stitching; if necessary, reposition to avoid your stitching undoing. See tip before you begin, then use a hole punch and remove the circle where marked. Place some fray stop around the edge of the holes and insert the eyelets as per the directions included with your installation tool.

Practise on spare fabric first if you're new to eyelets.

8. Weave ribbon through the eyelets and tie in a bow at the top. If you wish to keep the bow secure, you can hand sew a couple of stitches over it or add a small amount of craft glue.

9. Place the vinyl base rectangles on top of the background rectangles, with right sides together. Align the raw edges and sew them together along the base edge with a ¼in (6mm) seam allowance. Finger press the seam flat and topstitch with a ⅛in (3mm) seam allowance (*see Quilting & Finishing Techniques*).

10. Fold the short edges of the contrasting rectangles over ¼in (6mm), press with an iron and then repeat again to conceal the raw edges. Topstitch in place with a ⅛in (3mm) seam allowance.

11. Cut the webbing into two 12in (30cm) pieces and add fray stop to the raw edges. Find the centre of one contrasting rectangle, measure 1¾in (4.5cm) either side of it and mark with a fabric pen. Pin one piece of webbing at these markings, aligning the raw edges of the fabric with the raw edges of the webbing. Make sure your webbing isn't twisted! Place another rectangle on top, right sides together, sandwiching the webbing between the layers of fabric. Sew along the edge with a ¼in (6mm) seam allowance and fold along the stitching line so that the right sides of the two fabric rectangles are facing outwards. Press and topstitch with a ⅛in (3mm) seam allowance. Repeat to create two. This is now referred to as the drawstring compartment.

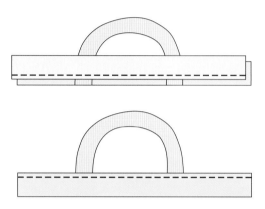

12. Position each drawstring compartment in the centre top of each background piece. Align the raw edges and tack (baste), using a ⅛in (3mm) seam allowance.

13. Place the prepared background pieces right sides together and sew around the sides and base. This is now referred to as the outer bag. Repeat this step for the lining, leaving a gap in one side.

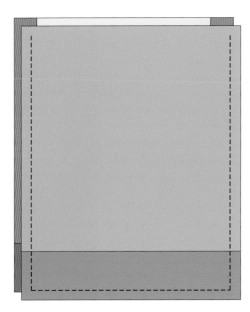

14. Turn the outer bag the right way out and place it inside the lining. Match up the side seams, pin and then sew completely around the top with a ⅜in (1cm) seam allowance. Turn the right way out through the gap left in the lining, and then sew the gap closed by hand or sewing machine.

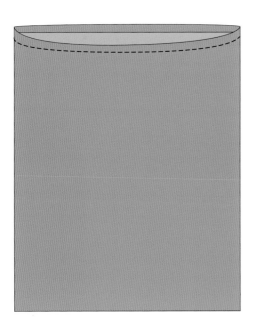

15. Ensure all the corners are pushed out nicely and give everything a press (avoiding the vinyl areas, of course!). Measure 1in (2.5cm) in from the bottom corners and 1in (2.5cm) in from the sides and mark for the grommet placement. These grommets will go through all layers of the backpack, so make sure the lining is pushed right to the corners. Use a hole punch and remove the circle where marked. Place some fray stop around the edge of the holes and insert grommets as per the directions included with the installation tool.

16. Cut the cord in half so that you have two lengths. Put sticky tape over the ends and push a safety pin through the end of the cord. Feed the cord through the left side of the drawstring compartment and out the other end, then through the other compartment (both ends on the left side). Bring the ends of the cord down and feed them through the grommet. Secure with a knot at the desired length. Repeat for the right side. Remove the sticky tape from the ends of the cord and fray below the knot to create a tasselled end.

Later, skater – you're ready to rock your new convertible backpack!

Koala Kool

Why does everyone invite ice cream to the party? Because it's COOL! Pack a picnic in this Aussie-inspired cooler bag, featuring a legenDAIRY Aussie koala-shaped chocolate ice cream along with floating glitter beneath the vinyl, and just chill out. Let's face it... life is better with sprinkles!

You will need

- **Machine feet:** Regular sewing foot, open toe foot and Teflon foot
- 15 x 22in (38 x 56cm) fabric, for background
- 15 x 22in (38 x 56cm) medium-weight woven fusible interfacing
- 15 x 44in (38 x 112cm) soft vinyl, for backing and sides
- 15 x 44in (38 x 112cm) reflective insulated batting (wadding) (*see Suppliers*), for lining
- 15 x 22in (38 x 56cm) clear vinyl
- 8in (20cm) square, fusible web
- 6 x 22in (15 x 56cm) cork fabric
- 6 x 22in (15 x 56cm) ultra-firm single-sided fusible stabilizer (*see Suppliers*)
- 6in (15cm) square, brown fabric, for koala
- Five 4in (10cm) squares, peach, coral, hot pink, citron and rust fabrics, for sticks, ice creams and koala nose
- 2½in (6cm) square, hot pink glitter vinyl

- 2in (5cm) square, pink wool felt, for koala mouth
- 34in (86cm) cotton webbing, 1½in (4cm) wide
- Two coconut buttons, ½in (12mm) diameter
- 12in (30cm) hook-and-loop fastener (Velcro), sew-in or heavy-duty adhesive, 1in (2.5cm) wide
- 2in (5cm) hook-and-loop fastener (Velcro), sew-in or heavy-duty adhesive, 1½in (4cm) wide
- Three glitter/sequin mixes
- Small funnel
- Sewing thread for construction
- Co-ordinating embroidery threads to match appliqué
- Double-sided tape, ¼in (6mm) wide
- Appliqué mat
- Air-erasable fabric marker
- Quilting clips

Finished size (excluding strap): 12 x 14in (30 x 35.5cm)

CUTTING INSTRUCTIONS

Soft vinyl
Cut one 12 x 14in (30 x 35.5cm) rectangle for the back.

Cut two 5½ x 14in (14 x 35.5cm) rectangles for the sides.

Reflective insulated wadding (batting)
Cut two 12 x 14in (30 x 35.5cm) rectangles for the front and back linings.

Cut two 5½ x 14in (14 x 35.5cm) rectangles for the side linings.

Cut one 5½ x 12in (14 x 30cm) rectangle for the base lining.

Cork fabric
Cut one 5½ x 12in (14 x 30cm) rectangle for the base.

Cut two 2½ x 7½in (6.5 x 19cm) rectangles for the closure.

Ultra-firm single-sided fusible stabilizer
Cut one 4½ x 11in (11.5 x 28cm) rectangle.

Background fabric and medium-weight woven fusible interfacing
Cut one 12 x 14in (30 x 35.5cm) rectangle of each.
Fuse the interfacing to the wrong side of the fabric.

Clear vinyl
Cut one 14 x 16in (35.5 x 40.5cm) rectangle.

1in (2.5cm) wide hook-and-loop fastener
Cut one 8in (20cm) piece.

Cut two 1in (2.5cm) pieces.

Cut one 1½in (4cm) piece, hook side only.

1½in (4cm) wide hook-and-loop fastener
Cut one 2in (5cm) piece, loop side only.

Often products like glitter vinyl, with a fabric backing, can be ironed gently from the back, but they should NEVER be ironed from the right side. Always test your product first before diving into your project.

CONSTRUCTION

1. Refer to *Modern Appliqué Techniques* at the beginning of this book and use the appliqué placement template provided to select your fabrics. Cut them out using the Koala Kool reversed appliqué pieces and the table below.

1, 4, 6	stick	peach fabric
2	ice cream base	coral fabric
3	ice cream top	hot pink fabric
5	ice cream	citron fabric
7, 8, 9	koala	brown fabric
10	nose	rust fabric
11	mouth	pink wool felt
12	heart	hot pink glitter vinyl or fabric

2. Use the *Layered Appliqué* instructions to construct units of the ice creams and koala following the number order shown. Use shapes 1–3 for the two-tone ice cream unit, shapes 4–5 for the other ice cream unit and shapes 6–11 for the koala unit.

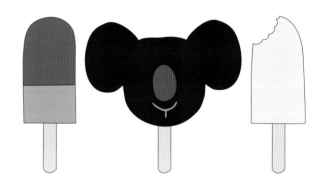

3. Position the completed ice cream appliqué units on the background fabric (portrait orientation) 1¼in (3cm) up from the baseline and about ¼in (6mm) apart (refer to the appliqué placement template). Fuse in place.

4. It's time to sew! Give your koala ice cream some texture with fun decorative stitches (see *Oh So Glam Decorative Stitching*). Use a cream thread to look like coconut! Refer to the list below as a guide for your stitch selection.

★ Ears: use a 1.5 x 3mm diagonal triple stitch.

★ Head: use a 4 x 4mm flower stitch.

★ Sticks, nose and ice creams: use a 2 x 2mm blanket stitch.

★ Mouth: use a 2mm straight stitch (felt doesn't fray).

5. Centre the clear vinyl on top of the appliquéd background; it is slightly bigger to make it easier to sew. Use some quilting clips to hold it in place. Change to a Teflon foot on your machine and set it to a 2mm straight stitch. Start on the straight edge of shape number 5 (the right-hand ice cream) and stitch around the edge of the shape, making sure you stop about 1in (2.5cm) before you reach the point where you started so that you can add your glitter/sequin mix.

6. Use a small funnel to insert the glitter/sequin mix. Fill as much or as little as you like – the more you add, the less of the fabric you'll see. Shake it down towards the sewn end and carefully finish stitching around the shape. Repeat this technique for shape numbers 3 (the other ice cream) and 10 (the koala nose).

7. Stitch around the edge of the background fabric with a ⅛in (3mm) seam allowance, then trim off any excess clear vinyl. Sew the button eyes on the koala.

8. Prepare the base by placing the piece of ultra-firm stabilizer fusible side down on the wrong side of the large piece of cork fabric. Centre and fuse carefully in place. With an air-erasable fabric marker, draw down the centre of the cork lengthwise and then draw lines 1in (2.5cm) either side. Sew down these three lines with a 3mm straight stitch to give the base more stability.

9. Lay the two 2½ x 7½in (6.5 x 19cm) pieces of cork fabric right side up. Position the heart appliqué on one piece of cork, approximately ½in (1cm) in from the short edge, and sew with a 2.5mm straight stitch. Adhere and/or stitch the 1½ x 2in (4 x 5cm) piece of hook-and-loop fastener on the other piece of cork, ½in (1cm) in from the short edge. Use double-sided tape to stick the two pieces of cork wrong sides together, ensuring that the heart and the hook-and-loop fastener are at the same end. Topstitch these pieces together with a ⅜in (1cm) seam allowance. With a rotary cutter and ruler, trim the seam allowance down to ¼in (6mm) to give a crisp finish. This is referred to as the closure unit.

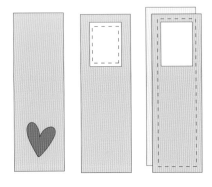

10. Lay the 12 x 14in (30 x 35.5cm) soft vinyl rectangle right side up (portrait orientation) and measure 9in (23cm) up from the bottom edge. Position the closure unit (the end without the heart appliqué) along this measurement. It is handy to use some double-sided tape at this end of the closure unit to hold it in place. Sew the closure unit into position by stitching a 1in (2.5cm) box.

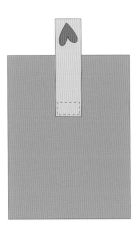

11. Lay the appliquéd rectangle right side up and measure 8in (20cm) up from the bottom edge. Position the 1 x 1½in (2.5 x 4cm) piece of hook-only fastener longways. Adhere and/or stitch in place.

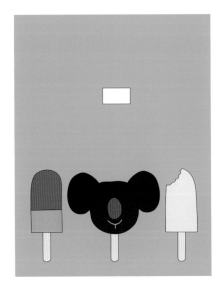

12. Adhere and/or stitch the remaining pieces of hook-and-loop fastener to the following pieces:

★ Soft vinyl side pieces: measure 1in (2.5cm) down from the top short edge and position 1in (2.5cm) hook-and-loop fastener pieces 1in (2.5cm) in from either side. Repeat for both soft vinyl side pieces.

★ Reflective insulated lining (front and back pieces): lay shiny side up (portrait orientation) and measure down 1in (2.5cm) from the top. Centre the 8in (20cm) piece of hook-and-loop fastener in the centre of each piece.

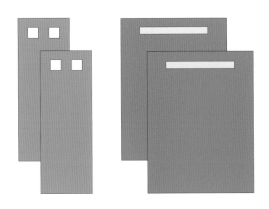

13. Place the two soft vinyl side pieces right side up. Turn these pieces so that the sides with the hook-and-loop fastener are facing towards each other. Lay the webbing on top, matching the raw edges of the webbing with the raw edges of the soft vinyl (the short edges without the hook-and-loop fastener). Pin the webbing in place. From each raw end of webbing, measure up 7in (18cm) and draw a line on the webbing with an air-erasable fabric marker. Topstitch the webbing in place from the raw edges up to the 7in (18cm) marking and back down to secure it to the vinyl.

14. Okay friends, gather all the pieces and let's put this together! Lay the cork base rectangle right side up and then position the appliquéd front rectangle right side down. Match up the bottom raw edges and stitch together with a ⅜in (1cm) seam allowance, but start and finish ⅜in (1cm) in from either end. Repeat to attach the soft vinyl back and side pieces, remembering to start and stop ⅜in (1cm) in from the edges. This is now referred to as the outer unit.

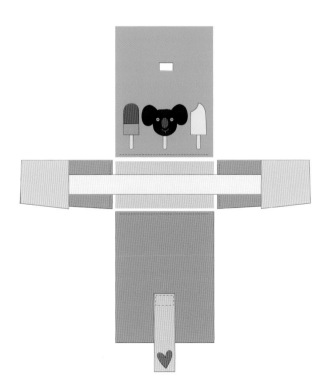

15. Align the side seams of the outer unit, matching the raw edges, pin/clip in place and stitch them together with a ⅜in (1cm) seam allowance.

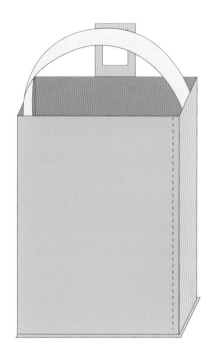

16. Repeat steps 14 and 15 for the reflective insulated lining pieces, leaving a gap of approximately 4in (10cm) in the middle of one side seam. This is now referred to as the lining unit.

17. Carefully clip the base corners and turn the outer unit the right way out. Place the outer unit inside the lining unit (right sides together), match the raw edges, and pin/clip together. Ensure the webbing strap and closure unit are out of the seam. Stitch completely around the top with a ⅜in (1cm) seam allowance.

18. Gently turn the right way out through the gap in the lining and then sew the hole closed. Double-sided tape makes this step a lot easier.

Now it's time to chill out and enjoy a picnic with your new insulated bag!

Totally Bee-licious

You'll BEE inspired to host your next dinner party with these gorgeous placemats! These happ-bee appliqués come together quickly and make the most perfect gift for any bee lover. Have fun creating crazy daisy combinations and get ready to BEE proud of your make.

You will need

- **Machine feet:** Open toe foot and regular sewing foot
- Four 18 x 44in (46 x 112cm) rectangles, brown, pink, yellow and orange fabrics, for background and backing
- One pack 16in (40.5cm) pre-cut round placemats (*see Suppliers*), or 32 x 44in (81 x 112cm) double-sided fusible interfacing
- 24 x 17in (61 x 43cm) fusible web
- Six 5 x 44in (12.5 x 112cm) strips, olive, mint, peach, tan, pink and red fabrics, for petals
- Three 5in (13cm) squares, pink, orange and peach fabrics, for centres
- Six 5in (13cm) squares, black and gold patterned fabrics, for bee body
- 10in (25cm) square, light blue fabric, for large wings
- 6in (15cm) square, blue fabric, for small wings
- 6½yd (6m) pre-made bias binding, 1in (2.5cm) wide
- Co-ordinating embroidery threads to match appliqué
- Sewing thread for construction to match background fabrics
- Appliqué mat

Finished size (set of 4): 16in (40.5cm) diameter

CUTTING INSTRUCTIONS

Background/backing fabrics

Cut two 18in (46cm) squares from each fabric. Fold them into quarters and position the 16in (40.5cm) quarter circle pattern piece provided on top, with the straight edges on the fold. If you don't have pre-cut double-sided fusible interfacing, you'll also need to cut four 16in (40.5cm) circles of interfacing. Ensure your ironing surface is protected. Fuse one circle of double-sided fusible interfacing to the wrong side of a background fabric circle. Repeat to create three more fused background circles. Note: leave the four backing circles off until after the appliqué is sewn.

CONSTRUCTION

1. Refer to *Modern Appliqué Techniques* at the beginning of this book and use the placement template provided to select your fabrics. Cut them out using the Totally Bee-licious reversed appliqué pieces and the table below.

1 (x6)	flower A petals	alternate olive & mint fabrics
2	flower A centre	pink fabric
1 (x6)	flower B petals	alternate peach & tan fabrics
2	flower B centre	orange fabric
1 (x6)	flower C petals	alternate red & pink fabrics
2	flower C centre	peach fabric
3, 4, 5, 6, 7, 8	bee body	black & gold fabrics
9, 11	large wings	light blue fabric
10, 12	small wings	blue fabrics

2. Use the *Basic Fusible Appliqué* instructions to construct units of the flowers and bees following the number order shown. Use shapes 1–2 for the A, B and C flower units and shapes 3–8 for the bee body unit.

3. Fuse each unit onto the prepared background circles.

4. It's time to sew! Refer to the list below as a guide for your stitch selection, and check out *Oh So Glam Decorative Stitching* at the beginning of this book.

★ Petals: 2.5mm x 2.5mm triple blanket stitch.

★ Centre: 4mm x 4mm decorative cross stitch pattern.

★ Bee piece 3: use a 'furry-look stitch, grass stitch or zigzag with approximately 4mm stitch width.

★ Bee piece 4: use a 3.5 x 3.5mm flower stitch.

★ Bee piece 5: use a 2 x 3mm (L x W) arrowhead decorative stitch.

★ Bee piece 6: use a 3 x 3mm cross stitch.

★ Bee piece 7: use a 2 x 4mm (L x W) feather stitch.

★ Bee piece 8: use a 1.5 x 4mm (L x W) triple zigzag stitch.

★ Antennae: use a 4 x 4mm flower stitch.

★ Wings: use a 2.5 x 2.5mm triple blanket stitch.

5. Fuse the remaining fabric backing circles to the back of the placements.

6. Using quilting clips, position the bias binding right side down on top of the placemat. Stitch the binding down with a ¼in (6mm) seam allowance. Fold the binding to the back and hand sew in place.

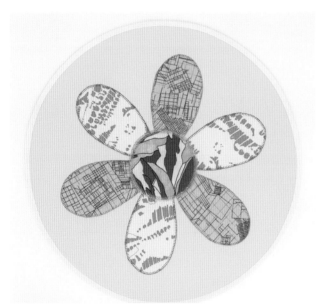

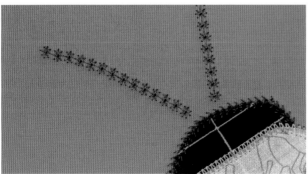

These bee-utiful placemats are ready for your next dinner party!

Prickly Positivi-tea

Aloe there! Did you get invited to the cacti tea party? I have no doubt it will be filled with only the best crazy cacti and loads of positivi-tea! You'll hear them chanting, 'You grow, girl! Stick with us, you'll be full of empowerment and feeling fan-cactus!'

You will need

- **Machine foot:** Teflon foot
- 20 x 22in (50 x 56cm) Osnaburg or natural linen fabric, for background
- 20 x 22in (50 x 56cm) fusible fleece
- 16 x 17in (40.5 x 43cm) fusible web
- Two 10in (25cm) squares, green and blue glitter vinyls, for cacti and rainbow
- 8in (20cm) square, pink/red fabric, for flowers
- Eight 6in (15cm) squares, bright patterned fabrics, for cacti details
- Six 4in (10cm) squares, solid fabrics, for rainbow and teacup details
- 10in (25cm) square, polka-dot fabric, for teapot
- 6in (15cm) square, pink patterned fabric, for teacup

- Co-ordinating embroidery threads to match appliqué
- Citron and peach embroidery threads, for quilting
- Sewing thread to match background fabric
- Fifteen medium pompoms
- 18in (46cm) diameter wooden embroidery hoop
- 10in (25cm) cord, for hanging
- Appliqué mat
- Fray stop
- Large quilting ruler
- Air-erasable fabric marker
- Glue stick or double-sided tape, ¼in (6mm) wide
- Craft glue

Finished size: 18in (46cm) diameter

CUTTING INSTRUCTIONS

Osnaburg/linen fabric and fusible fleece

Cut one 20in (50cm) square of each and fuse the fleece to the wrong side of the fabric. This will be referred to as the background fabric.

Vinyl isn't your thing? No worries, babe – you can totally use regular fabric as an alternative.

CONSTRUCTION

1. Refer to *Modern Appliqué Techniques* at the beginning of this book and use the placement template provided to select your fabrics. Cut them out using the Prickly Positivi-tea reversed appliqué pieces and the table below.

1, 2, 3, 14	flowers	pink/red fabric
4, 15	large & small cactus	green glitter vinyls
5, 6, 7, 8, 9, 16, 17, 18	cacti detail	variety of bright patterned fabrics
10	teapot	polka-dot printed fabric
11, 12, 19, 20, 22, 23	rainbow & teacup details	solid fabrics
13	rainbow	blue glitter vinyl or fabric
21	teacup	pink patterned fabric

2. Use the *Basic Fusible Appliqué* instructions to construct units of the cacti, rainbow and teacup in the number order shown. Use a glue pen to hold any glitter vinyl elements in place, and do not iron the vinyl from the right side. Use shapes 1–9 for the large cactus unit, shapes 11–13 for the rainbow, shapes 14–18 for the small cactus unit and shapes 19–23 for the teacup.

3. Once you have prepared the above units, fuse the cacti, teapot and teacup together on the appliqué mat, starting from shape number 1 and building the units up until you reach shape number 23. This is now referred to as the cacti unit. Once cool, remove the appliqué from the mat in one piece.

4. Using a quilting ruler and fabric marker, draw 1in (2.5cm) vertical guides on the background fabric. It's time to quilt (*see Quilting & Finishing Techniques*). Add interest to the background with some decorative stitch quilting (*see Oh So Glam Decorative Stitching*).

Use the following as a guide.

★ Citron thread: using a 1.5 x 4mm (L x W) zigzag triple stitch, stitch two lines and leave a space between for a different colour.

★ Peach thread: using a 2 x 3mm (L x W) arrowhead decorative stitch, stitch the remaining lines in between the citron ones.

6. Position the cacti unit in the centre of the quilted background and fuse in place, being careful of the vinyl. Use glue or double-sided tape to hold the cacti.

7. Give your cacti a spikey texture with fun decorative stitches – check out *Oh So Glam Decorative Stitching*. Contrast some threads with the fabric and make the stitching POP! Use the following as a guide.

★ Cacti: use a 4 x 4mm cross stitch.

★ Teapot: use a 3 x 3mm flower stitch.

★ Cacti details, flowers, rainbow and teacup: use a 2 x 2mm blanket stitch.

8. Undo the wooden embroidery hoop, lay the fabric over the inner circle frame and position the outer frame over, sandwiching the fabric between. Tighten the top screw of the hoop and pull as taut as you can. Leave an approximately 2in (5cm) seam allowance around the circle and trim off any excess. Apply fray stop to the ends of the decorative stitching where it runs off the edge of the fabric to prevent it from coming undone.

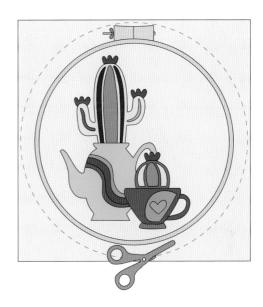

9. With a hand sewing needle and thread, sew a gathering stitch around the edge of the excess fabric, pull and secure tightly.

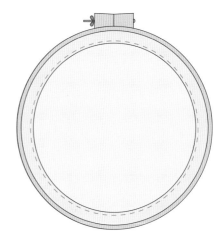

10. Tie a piece of cord at the top of your hoop art and glue pompoms around the outer edge of the embroidery hoop.

Celebrate your spikey creation!

Templates

These reversed appliqué pieces are all shown at actual size. Printable versions, and SVG versions (for use with electronic cutting machines), can be downloaded from www.davidandcharles.com.

Otterly Adorable

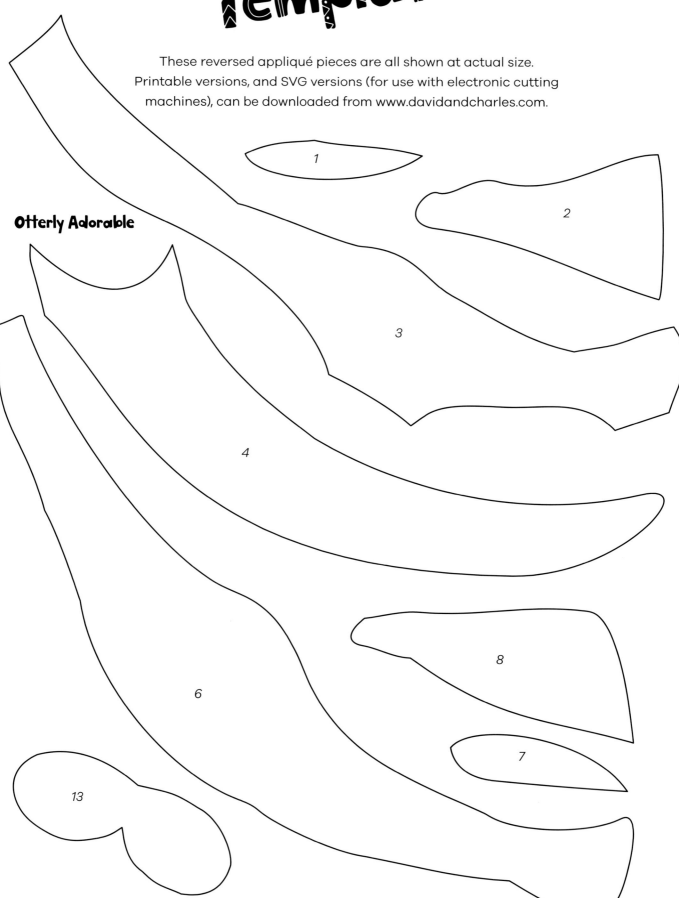

Hanging with My Gnomies

Animals x 4

Join here

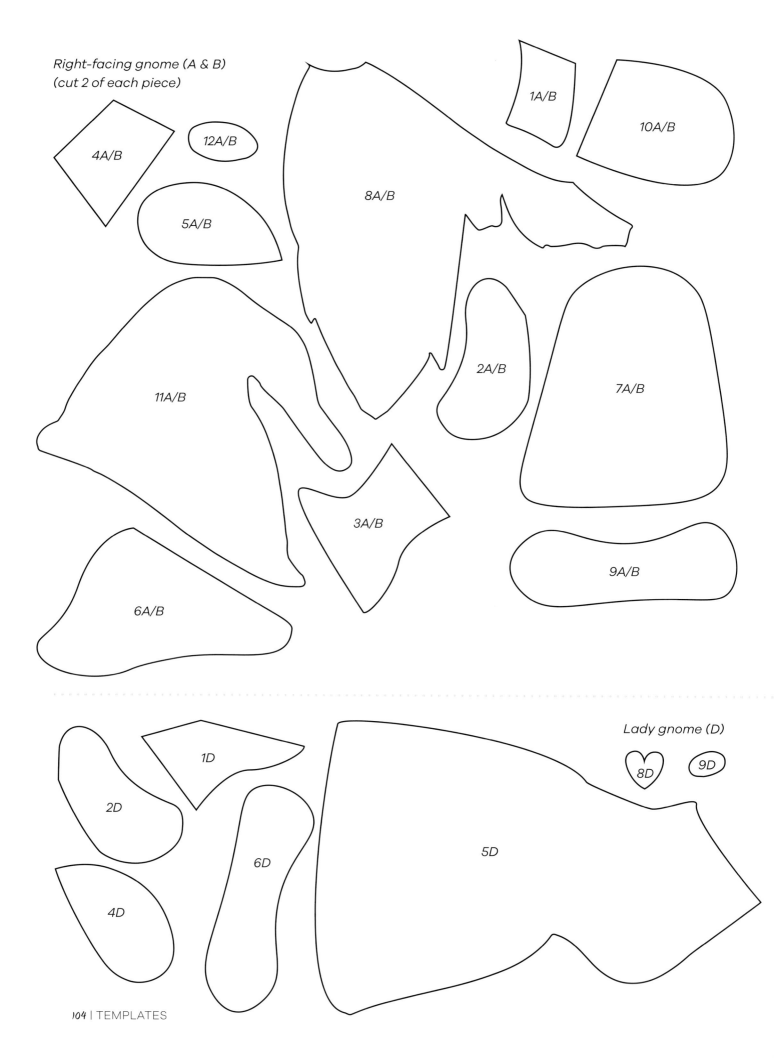

Right-facing gnome (A & B)
(cut 2 of each piece)

4A/B

12A/B

5A/B

8A/B

1A/B

10A/B

11A/B

2A/B

7A/B

3A/B

6A/B

9A/B

Lady gnome (D)

1D

2D

6D

4D

8D

9D

5D

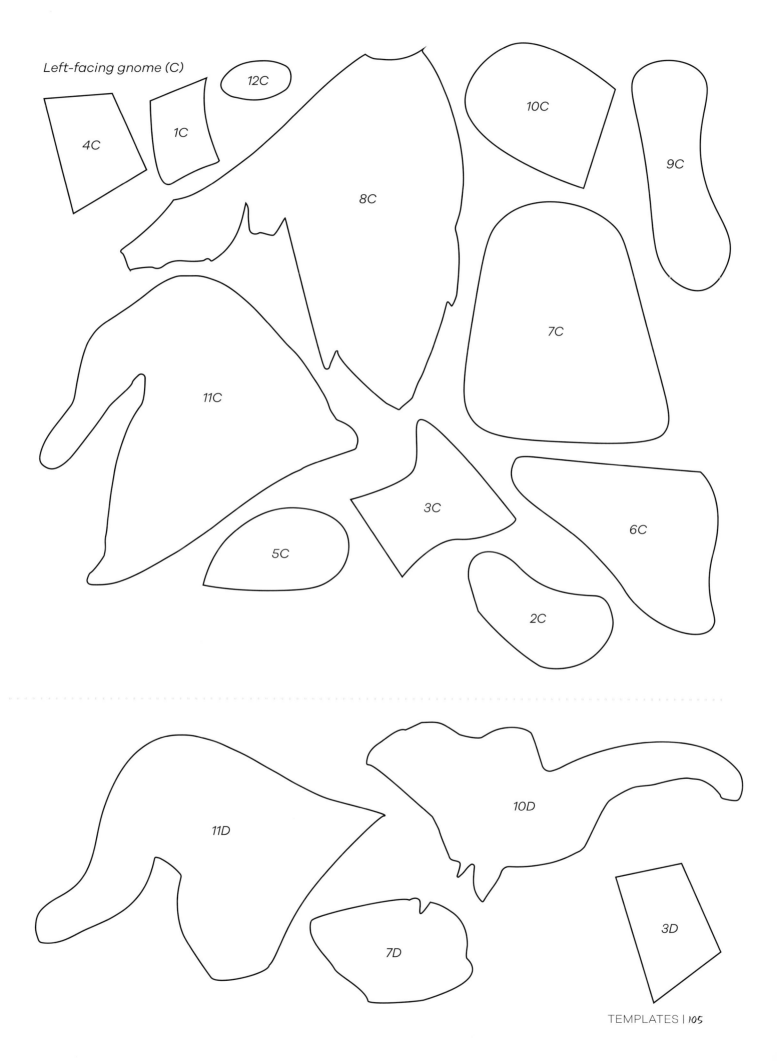

Left-facing gnome (C)

12C

4C

1C

10C

9C

8C

10D

7C

11C

5C

3C

6C

2C

11D

10D

7D

3D

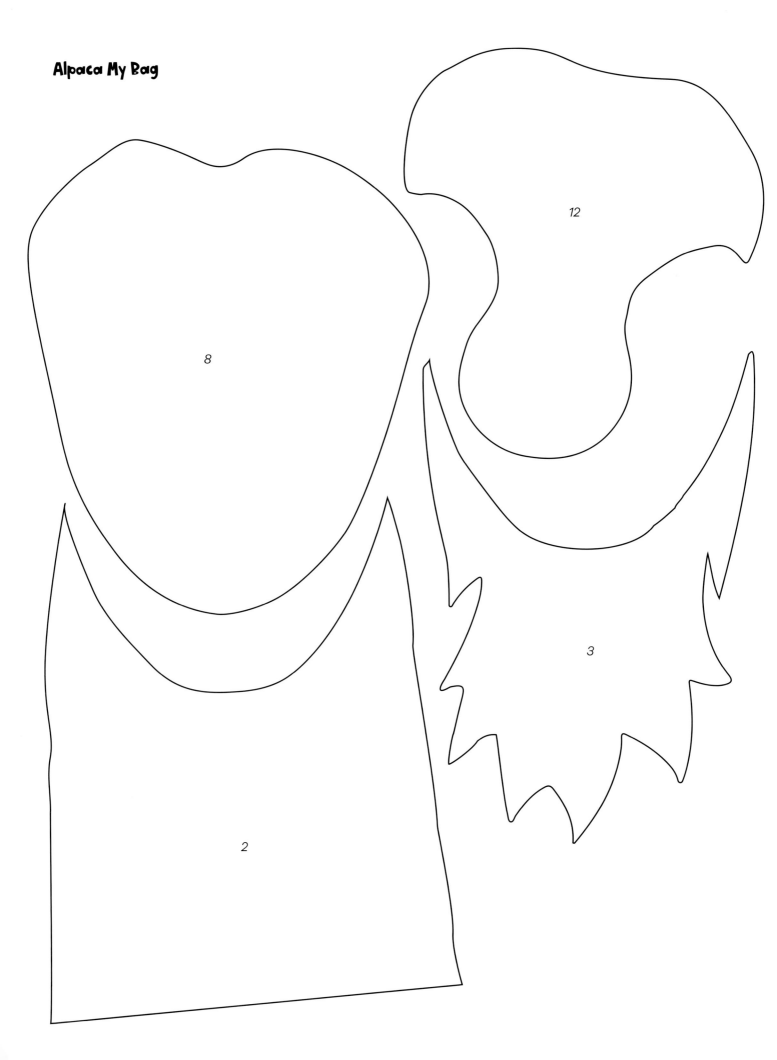

Alpaca My Bag

Life's Short, Eat Donuts!

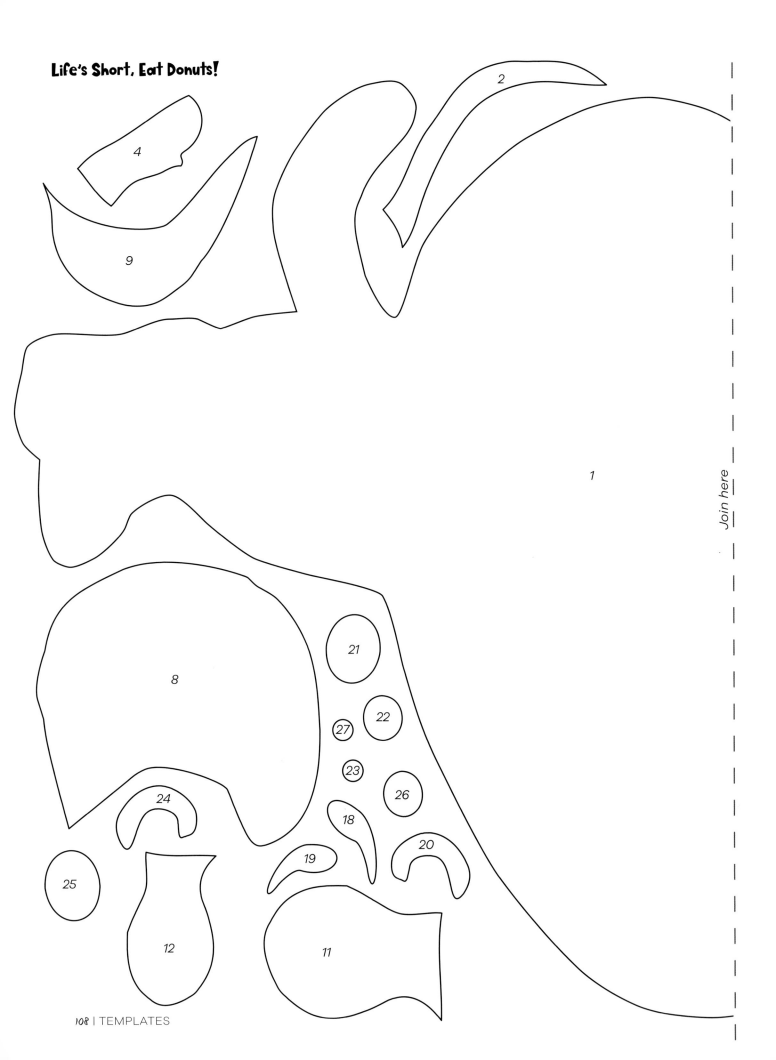

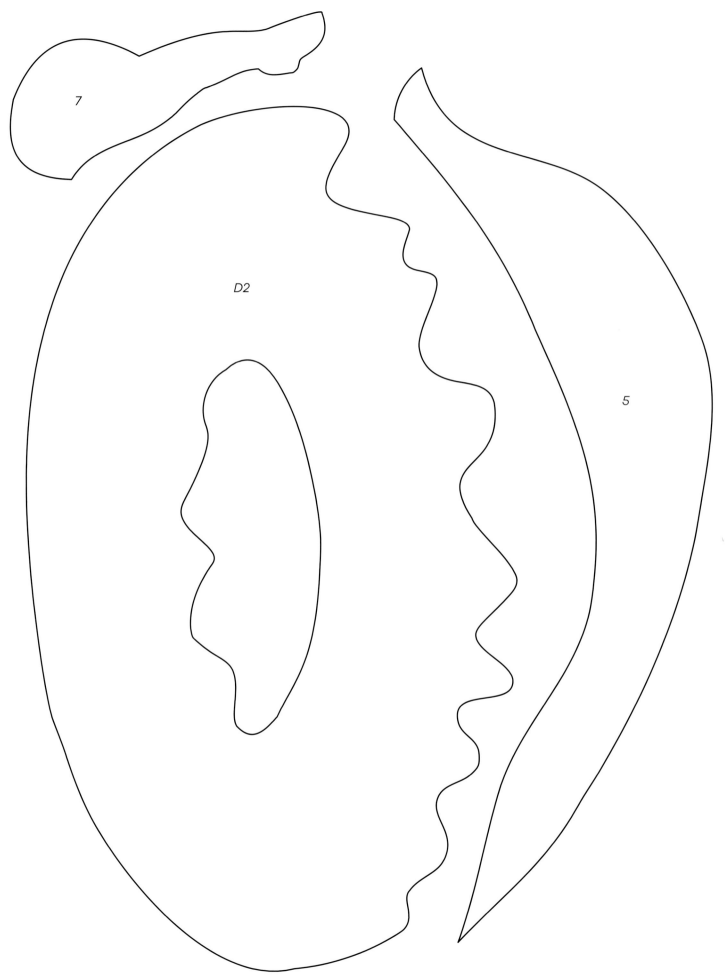

7

D2

5

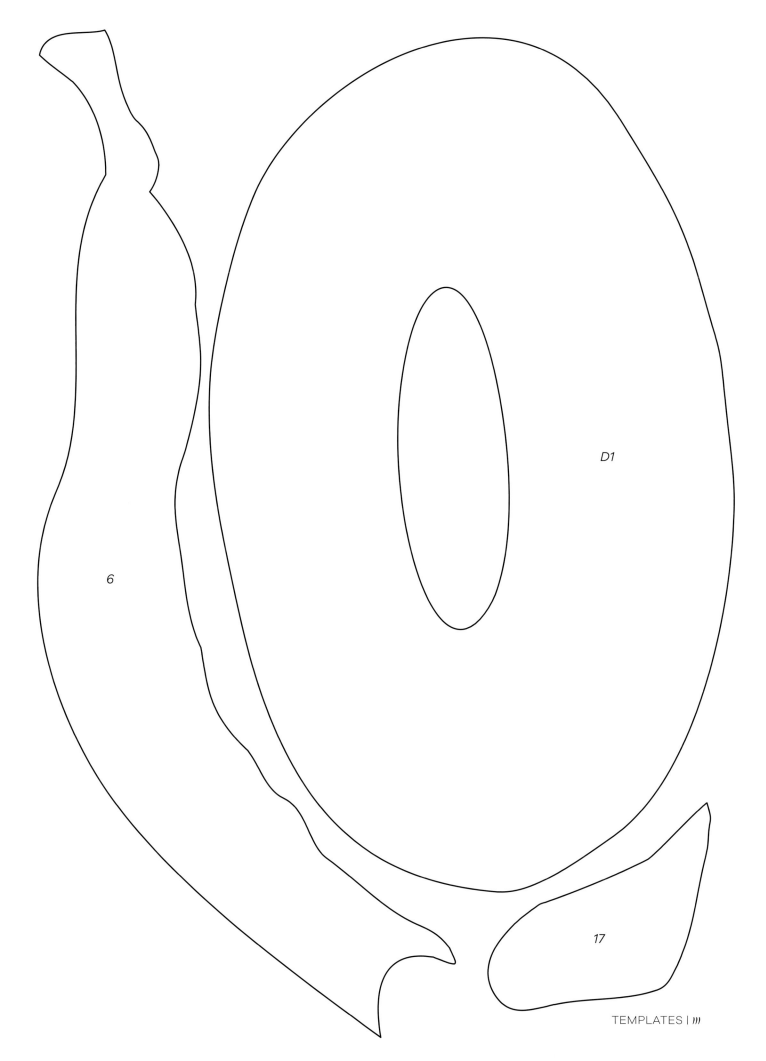

D1

6

17

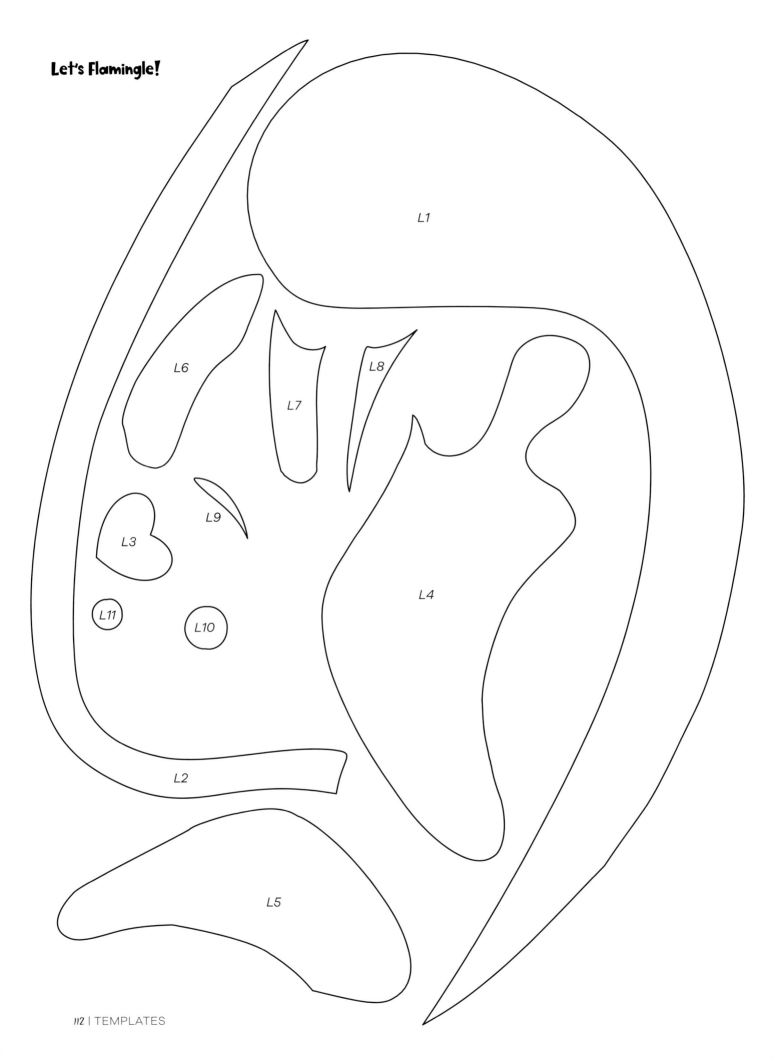

Let's Flamingle!

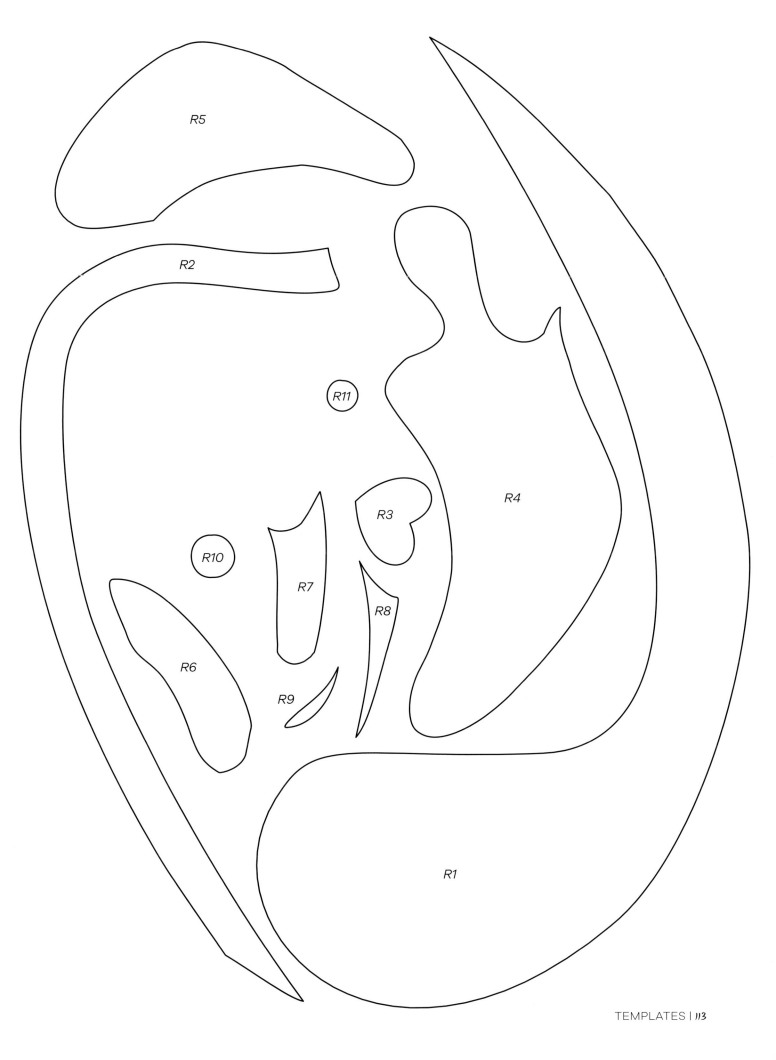

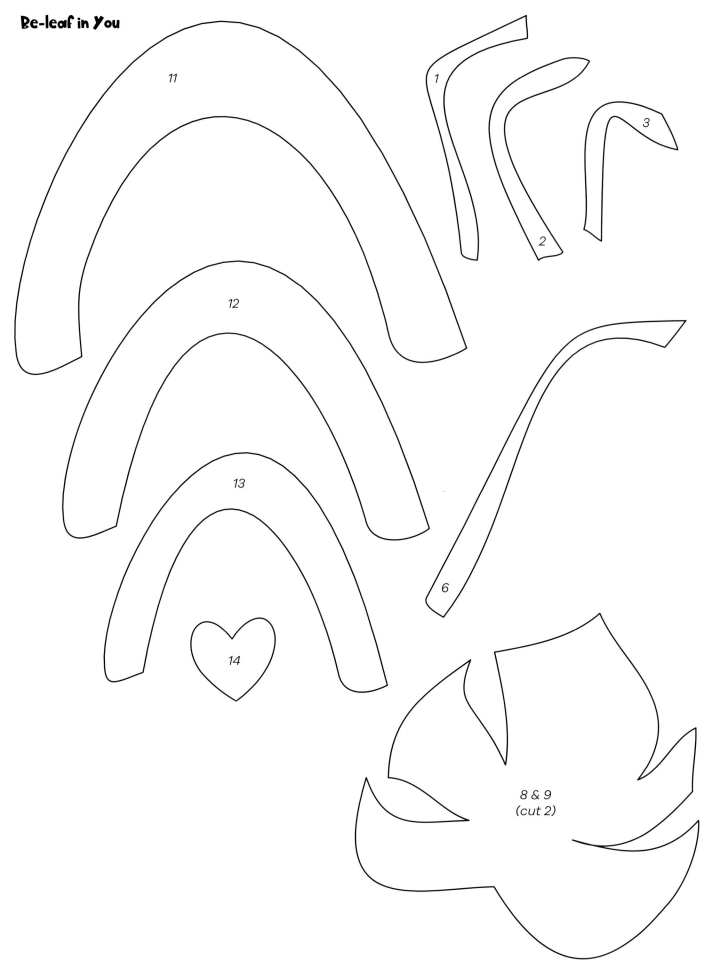

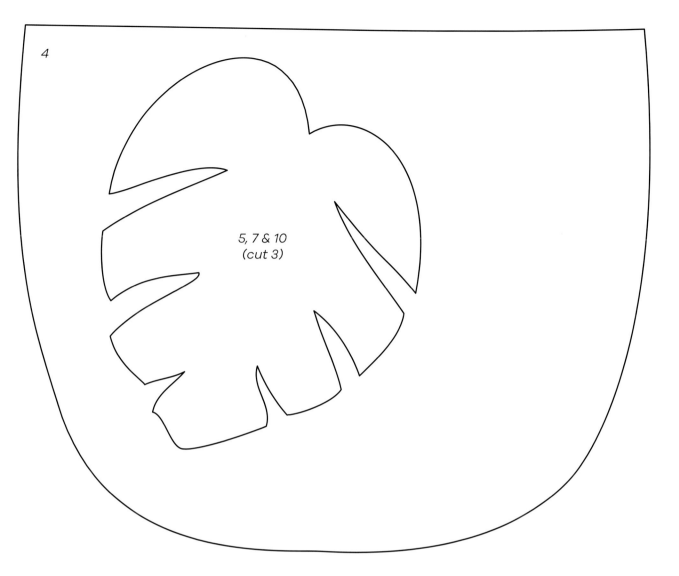

4

5, 7 & 10
(cut 3)

Koala Kool

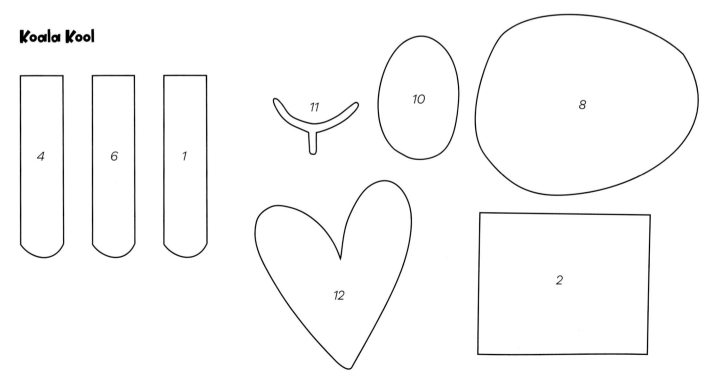

4

6

1

11

10

8

12

2

Koala Kool Bag continued

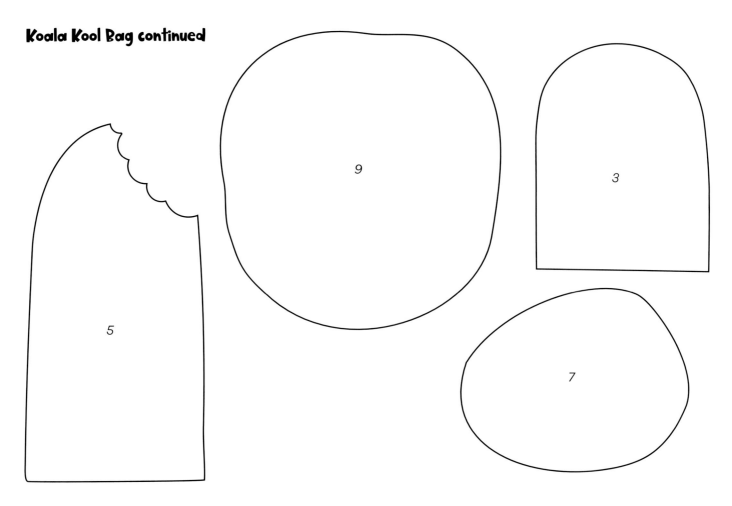

5

9

3

7

Totally Bee-licious

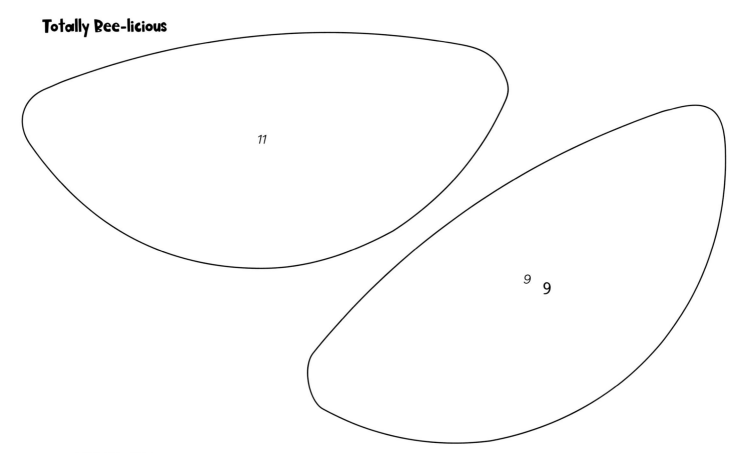

11

9 9

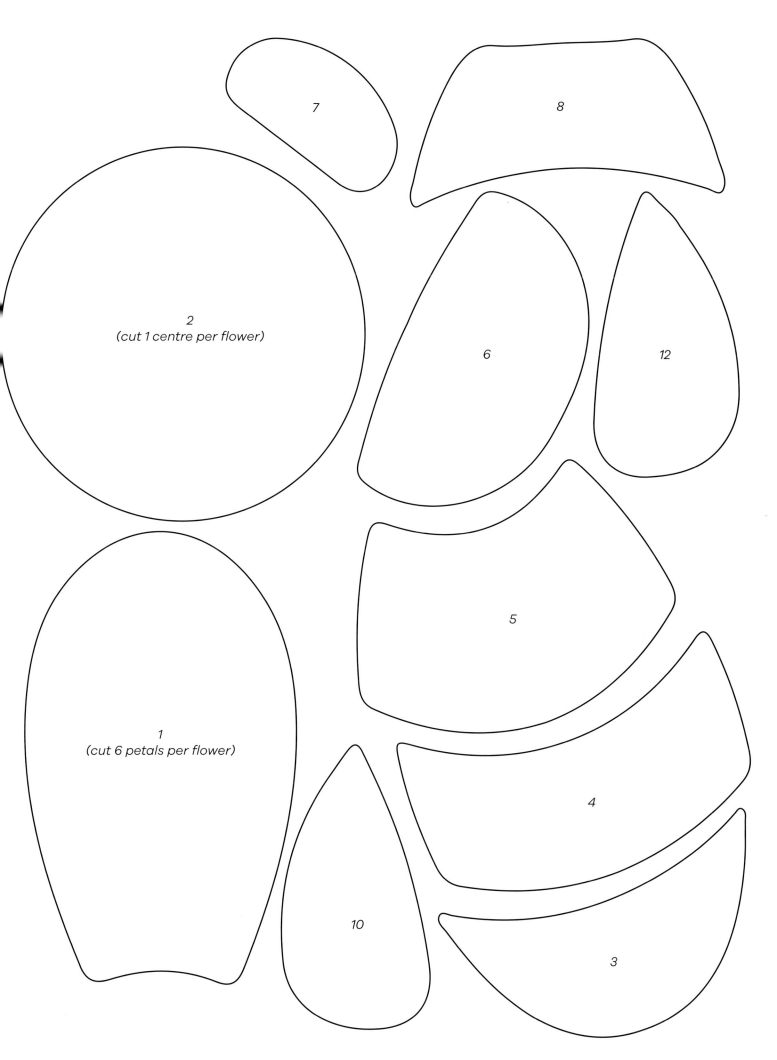

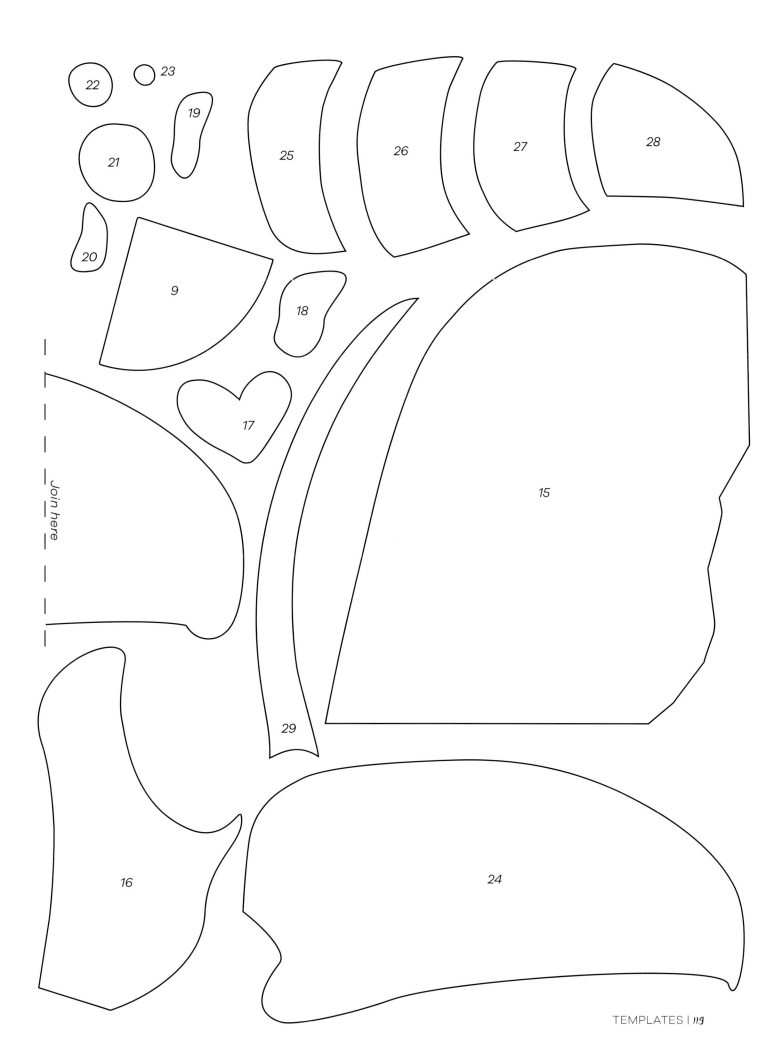

22

23

19

21

20

9

18

25

26

27

28

Join here

17

15

29

16

24

You are Dino-Mite!

Rad and Fab

6

19

11

18

10

20

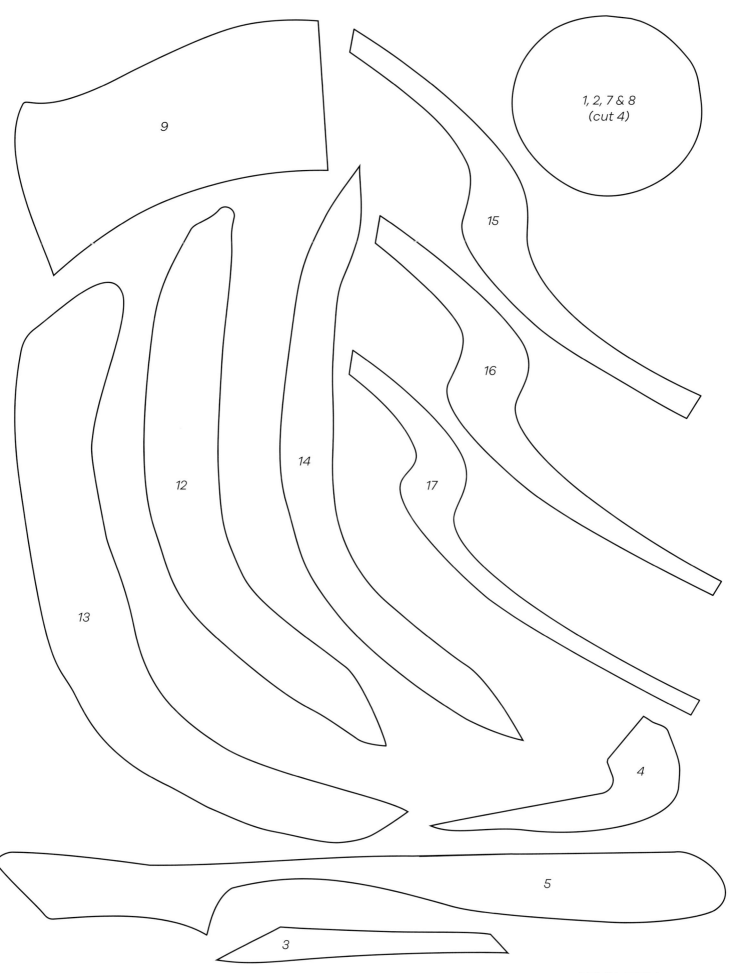

Prickly Positivi-tea

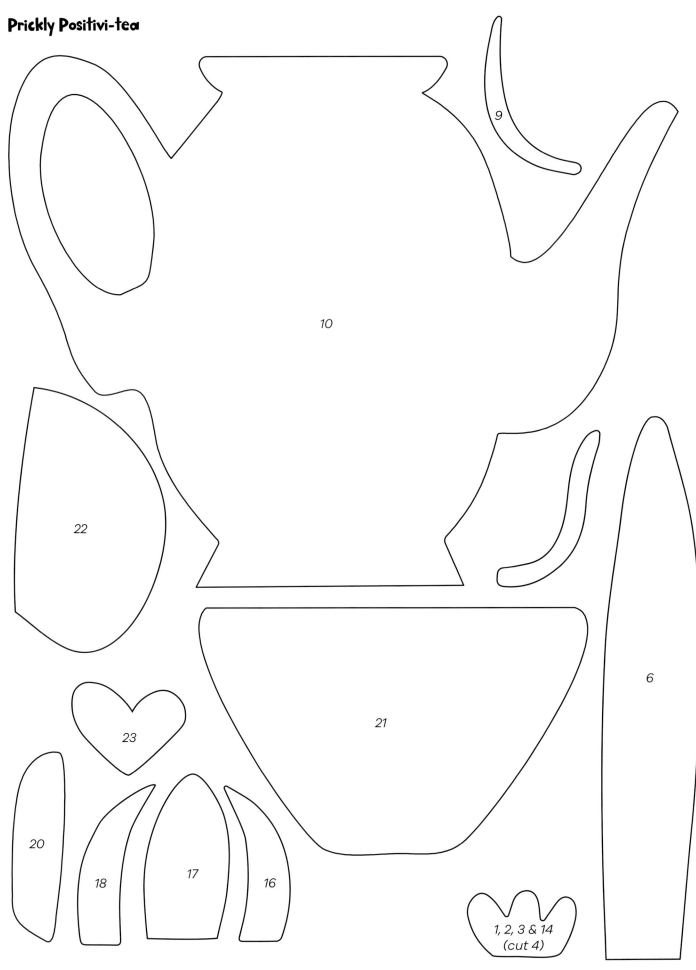

9

10

22

6

23

21

20

18

17

16

1, 2, 3 & 14
(cut 4)

About the Author

Mandy is the creator, teacher and inspirer behind the brand, Sew Quirky. She enables creative opportunities through her sewing patterns, online tutorials and workshops around the world. Mandy fills her students with confidence and empowerment in a celebration of their creative achievements. Recognized as a Bernina and Bernette ambassador in Australia, Mandy enjoys working with brands that align with her focus on nurturing the next generation of sewers. Taking any opportunity to make people smile, Mandy's designs are renowned for their colour, texture and character.

Join this fairy-bread loving Aussie and her sidekick, Toby the Jack Russell, for a stroll in their wonderful world of appliqué and textile art. Say G'day to Mandy on one of her social platforms below! Tag Mandy in your finished and in-progress projects on Instagram or in the Sew Quirky VIP Group on Facebook. Let's celebrate YOUR amazing creations!

★ **Instagram:** @sewquirky

★ **Facebook:** @sewquirky.au

★ **Website:** sewquirky.com.au

★ **YouTube:** youtube.com/c/SewQuirky

★ **Pinterest:** pinterest.com.au/SewQuirky1/

Thank you!

A massive shout out to all the people in my tribe who have brought this book to life.

To my beautiful mumma Leanne, and my lovely daddo Max, you guys are one awesome support crew – listening to my ideas, reading countless patterns, helping me finish samples and always being there for me when I need you. You're amazing! My lil bro Cody, thank you for your coffee and food delivery service at the drop of a hat when I needed a pick-me-up. You're a little legend. My sweet sis Kate, your thoughtful and encouraging words are always appreciated. You all have shaped me into the character I am today, and I am so proud of us all. We are always growing together and always making new memories. We are one awesome family unit. Thank you for everything you do for me.

My amazing man Nick, you have supported me endlessly. I am so grateful to have you by my side. You always believe in my crazy ideas and encourage me to keep going, to chase my dreams and reach them. You are one-of-a-kind. From our early high school years together and beyond, you continue to fill my life with your love, helpfulness and kindness.

To my gorgeous friends... my buddies, you guys are seriously amazing. Thank you so much for understanding my lack of free time while I was focusing on this book. You made phone calls count, filling them with positive reinforcement and motivation. A particular shout-out to these beautiful souls who went above and beyond with their encouragement and support: Caroline, Kimmy, Kylie, Lizzy, Penny and Sam, thank you for reassuring me with loads of, 'you've got this'! Thanks buddies!

A big thank you to Jane Trollope, Sarah Callard, Jeni Chown and all of the incredible creative team who have helped bring this book to life. You believed in me and now I get to share my vision and projects with the world.

Lastly, to my community of makers and shakers. Thank you for giving me the opportunities to pass on my knowledge and inspire you to create your own amazing works of art with my patterns. You are always positive and loaded with support that never goes unnoticed; it is forever appreciated. You guys rock!

Suppliers

Check out the Sew Quirky website at **sewquirky.com.au** for loads of appliqué supplies, zippers, cork and vinyls. You can visit your local quilting or department stores for supplies too. You can also ask your local quilting store to stock Sew Quirky patterns, continuous zippers, supplies and my ultra clear SQ appliqué mat. Here I've listed some alternative online retailers for key supplies that you'll need for the projects in this book:

Fusible web, stabilizers, fabrics and trims

★ michaels.com

★ joann.com

★ spotlight.com.au

★ hobbycraft.co.uk

★ amazon.com

★ etsy.com

Vinyls, cork, zippers and bag hardware

★ sewquirky.com.au

★ sewhot.co.uk

★ sallietomato.com

★ whosayssew.com

★ themodernsew.ist

★ keepsakequilting.com

★ hungryhippiesew.com

★ watergirlquiltco.com

★ madaboutpatchwork.com

Index

A DAVID AND CHARLES BOOK
© David and Charles, Ltd 2021

David and Charles is an imprint of David and Charles, Ltd
Suite A, Tourism House, Pynes Hill, Exeter, EX2 5WS

Text and Designs © Mandy Murray 2021
Layout and Photography © David and Charles, Ltd 2021

First published in the UK and USA in 2021

Mandy Murray has asserted her right to be identified as author of this work in
accordance with the Copyright, Designs and Patents Act, 1988.

All rights reserved. No part of this publication may be reproduced in any form or by any means, electronic or
mechanical, by photocopying, recording or otherwise, without prior permission in writing from the publisher.

Readers are permitted to reproduce any of the designs in this book for their
personal use and without the prior permission of the publisher. However, the designs
in this book are copyright and must not be reproduced for resale.

The author and publisher have made every effort to ensure that all the instructions
in the book are accurate and safe, and therefore cannot accept liability for any
resulting injury, damage or loss to persons or property, however it may arise.

Names of manufacturers and product ranges are provided for the information
of readers, with no intention to infringe copyright or trademarks.

A catalogue record for this book is available from the British Library.

ISBN-13: 9781446308820 paperback
ISBN-13: 9781446380949 EPUB

This book has been printed on paper from approved suppliers and made from pulp from sustainable sources.

Printed in China by Asia Pacific for:
David and Charles, Ltd
Suite A, Tourism House, Pynes Hill, Exeter, EX2 5WS

10 9 8 7 6 5 4 3 2 1

Publishing Director: Ame Verso
Senior Commissioning Editor: Sarah Callard
Managing Editor: Jeni Chown
Project Editor: Jane Trollope
Proofreader: Sarah Hoggett
Head of Design: Sam Staddon
Design and Art Direction: Laura Woussen
Pre-press Designer: Ali Stark
Illustrations: Kuo Kang Chen
Photography: Jason Jenkins
Production Manager: Beverley Richardson

David and Charles publishes high-quality books on a wide range of subjects.
For more information visit www.davidandcharles.com.

Share your makes with us on social media using #dandcbooks and
follow us on Facebook and Instagram by searching for @dandcbooks.

Layout of the digital edition of this book may vary depending on reader hardware and display settings.